BOOKS BY ABBIE HOFFMAN

Fuck the System

Revolution for the Hell of It

Woodstock Nation

Steal This Book

Vote!
(with Jerry Rubin and Ed Sanders)

To America with Love
(with Anita Hoffman)

The Autobiography of Abbie Hoffman
(formerly *Soon to Be a Major Motion Picture*)

Square Dancing in the Ice Age

Steal This Urine Test
(with Jonathan Silvers)

The Best of Abbie Hoffman

by Free

FOREWORD BY HARVEY WASSERMAN

INTRODUCTION BY REVEREND BILLY

THUNDER'S MOUTH PRESS
NEW YORK

REVOLUTION FOR THE HELL OF IT

AVALON
publishing group incorporated

Published by
Thunder's Mouth Press
An Imprint of Avalon Publishing Group
245 West 17th Street, 11th Floor
New York, NY 10011

First Thunder's Mouth Press edition April 2005

Library of Congress Cataloging-in-Publication Data is available.

ISBN: 1-56025-690-7

9 8 7 6 5 4 3 2 1

Printed in the United States
Distributed by Publishers Group West

Dedicated to FREE

CONTENTS

FOREWORD

Abbie! Abbie!! Abbie!!! Where the hell are you, goddammit?!?

Revolution for the Hell of It, indeed.

You yelled about "isms" being "wasms." If *Hell of It* was an ism, it'd be an anarchist. But you wouldn't stand for that. Such a label would be too conventional. You understood inside and out—Brandeis baccalaureate and all that good academic stuff—what these isms really were, and how they could be used in their time and place. And you knew that they may have still had this or that to offer. But having taken far more than your share of acid, you also knew that they were *boring* and it was time for something new.

Smart guy is an understatement. Street smart. Book smart. Media smart. People smart. Smart enough to help stop a war. Sly enough to drag the TV nets around on a string. Brave enough to stand up to the clubs, the guns, the nuts, the thugs, the prudes.

Count how many times in this book you get beat up. How many flings onto filthy jail floors. How many hours in court. How many nasty nights in those dank, dark hoosegows you treat so lightly in print.

A pool hustle this book is. Like you say somewhere toward the back: you don't have to beat everybody, just the one you're playing at the time. But you don't open with that, do you?

And you beat a lot of them.

You marched in the South, earnest and liberal, just out of college. It was the early sixties. They're not mentioned here, but you had a wife and a couple of kids back then. What were the costs of jumping away from all that?

A college degree. A master's in psychology (wouldn't *that* come in handy!). Short hair, shirt, a tie. I've seen the pictures. You could've been a prof or a shrink. Wrote great books. Billed big. Established institutes. Run asylums. Smoked a pipe (well . . . you did do a lot of that).

Instead, you went south (as did your income). You went to Georgia where they hung nosy Jew-boys like you. You went to Mississippi where they buried carpetbagging freedom riders in earthen levees, then waited forty years to charge the Klansmen who did it. You were around to see Ronald Reagan kick off his presidential campaign there.

But you had that, what? Jewish conscience? Sense of history? Righteous anger? Willful wanderlust? And guts of iron. And balls of steel.

Brains? No doubt about those. And among the many things you taught was that the greatest way to learn history is to make it. And the greatest kick—the one after the LSD and free love and media ego-blasts and dancing in the streets—is the sense of being in the vortex of social change. The joy of winning good, righteous victories for truth, justice, and the American way. You surfed history the way Hawaiians ride those big curls on the North Shore—shouting ecstatic all the way—except you helped create the waves you rode and loved almost every minute of it. Almost.

It's that love that made you a living revolution. But there's plenty of hell between the lines. You beat them all . . . almost.

HUAC . . . that vile, feared, bigoted, small-minded cancerous witch hunt that terrorized the liberals of the fifties . . . you and Jerry mocked it to death in a single stroke with your 1776 costumes and shouts of "Theater!!" in a crowded fire. Gutsy genius that was. Wild, brilliant, supremely savvy, and breathtakingly brave that was. How many years could they have put you away for? How many decades of lobotomous repression did you exorcise?

LBJ . . . that tragic Texan who just couldn't let go of a war he couldn't win and dragged this nation into hell because of it. He quit rather than face four more years of the likes of incomprehensible, incorrigible, and unbeatable street suburbanurchins like you who could run rings around his bleeding, tortured self. Sad for us all he left only after deciding to escalate a war in Vietnam that continues to ravage what's left of this nation, injecting a poisonous cancer into our soul that has eaten away our economy, our environment, our schools, our faith, and our democracy until we are left with the dregs of the draft-dodging W (for worthless) whom you would have despised beyond all reason and for all the right reasons.

Why we miss you now more than ever, Abbie, is maybe you would have had an answer for these despicable self-righteous anti-Christ know-nothing barbarians. That would have been a debate for the ages. Forget the Yippie-Yuppie stuff. How about Abbie v. W.

What would you have told us, dear brother? How would you have beaten them?

There are answers galore in this *Revolution for the Hell of It*.

No mere period piece, this. It opens with a stunning stoned ramble, a walk on Abbie's wild side, a stream of conscious chest beating LSD-inspired Hello complete with an acid rap on "phony words" and the juxtaposition of the words of Che with an ad for laundry soap. Then ranting (rightly) at Radio Havana for playing crap music.

I remember an older Abbie continuing to carry on two decades later. By then he could have been selling insurance already. Or coming over for dinner to share a radical uncle's armchair antiwar stories as the kids nod off with knowing yawns.

That wasn't for Abbie. In the eighties, we spoke together at Temple University with Bobby Seale, who was then writing a cookbook. Abbie was still cooking revolution, this time of the no nukes variety. No aging. No aching knees. This dude was still all elbows.

He called my mother to discuss recipes for chicken soup. Then he helped President Carter's daughter Amy get busted protesting the CIA—and get off from it, getting the spy meisters barred from campuses altogether. He did it all with the same verve and genius with which he navigated the terminal tsunami of a doomed imperial war.

What the Yippies did in Chicago was a pivot point in history whose importance is impossible to overstate.

What Abbie left us in this book is not merely the game plan of a supreme organizer, social critic, and comic genius. It's also a documentary dissection of one of the most important events of our lifetimes.

From 1932 to 1968 the Democratic Party of Franklin Roosevelt and Harry Truman, Adlai Stevenson and John Kennedy, Lyndon

Johnson and Hubert Humphrey, had dominated American politics. In the eight years of Ike (1953–61) the Dems still mostly dominated Congress. But the Republicans of the day would now qualify as moderate Democrats. Many of them had consciences and intellects. They could distinguish true morality from pompous psuedoreligious psychosis, and embraced the New Deal, from which Abbie stemmed in spades (or, as he puts it in here, *with* the spades).

What killed the Democrats was not Abbie or we Yippies running through the streets of Chicago while the whole world watched. Because what the whole world really saw was the Democrats' lethal embrace of all that we hated—the hypocrisy, the arrogance, and, most importantly, the Cold and Vietnam Wars, which a new generation would not tolerate, and which gutted this nation morally and spiritually, economically and ecologically.

Some on the left now blame Abbie and his Yippie ilk for stripping the liberals away from Hubert Humphrey in 1968 and handing the election to Richard Nixon, a blow from which the Democrats have never recovered.

But it's bullshit. What killed the Democrats in 1968 and ever since was their unwillingness to make hard, clear choices. George Wallace cracked their solid South, which they'd held since Andrew Jackson based on slavery and racism. Even FDR wouldn't challenge the power of southern bigotry. Then the Democrats put that final bullet in their head with the supremely suicidal contraction of allegedly starting to court southern black votes here while slaughtering Asians in Vietnam and crushing revolution—or even reform—in Africa, Latin America, and elsewhere.

In 1964, Abbie and a few of his ilk—like another departed brother named Marshall Bloom, who later founded the legendary Liberation News Service—were already making themselves felt in the segregated South. LBJ told Martin Luther King at MLK's 1964 Nobel Prize ceremony that the president of the United States couldn't guarantee the right of African-American citizens to vote. So they marched on Selma and lit up the South. When they got the Voting Rights Act and the guarantee of one person, one vote, the whites like Wallace blamed the Democrats and the solid South was on its way from the Party of Jackson to the Klan of Reagan-Bush.

But if the Dems had any of Abbie's guts and convictions, it would have been otherwise. President Hoffman would have withdrawn immediately from Vietnam and supported people of color in their revolutions (while putting better music on their radio broadcasts). He would have united the white followers of Elvis with the blacks from whom his music derived.

It's all here in *Revolution for the Hell of It*. A Yiddishe bochur who goes down to a police station where "spades" are being unjustly held and kicks in a trophy case to get himself arrested.

Yeah, he was young and tough and not a little crazy. But so was Ethan Allen and those yippie Green Mountain Boys. Sam Adams and those Digger Minutemen who turned Boston Harbor into a teapot. Big Bill Haywood and those wacky Wobblies. Emma Goldman and Margaret Sanger, Gene Debs and Pete Seeger, Dorothy Day and Saul Alinsky . . . Abbie learned from them all, then threw in some living theater and Marshall McLuhan, some Dali and Lenny Bruce . . . and . . . YIPPIE!!

Abbie could have told the Democrats to live by their convictions . . . and lighten up. My own whack on the ass in Chicago could have been worse. While he laughed at tanks on Michigan Avenue, Lissa and I got smacked up against a wall right next to a plate glass window that crashed in on unsuspecting dinner guests who got doused with our communal hit of tear gas.

But far worse happened to the Democrats. Not until Bill Clinton, who had his own touch of Yippie (but he blew it), did they see their desperate need for Abbie-style humor and cultural hipness. Had Clinton had some of Abbie's courage and conviction to go along with that media magic and scoundrel's verve, the hell of Bush-Rove and their fundamentalist firing squad might have stayed sunk in the cesspool of phony religion and corporate kleptocracy.

And then, of course, they forgot it again while Gore and Kerry put us all to sleep and opened the door for the anti-Christ.

But for far too long liberal America has cried out for the rebirth of a genius media guerilla. From Humphrey to McGovern to Carter to Carter to Mondale to Dukakis to Clinton to Clinton to Gore to Kerry it's been dull dull dull dull dull dull Clinton Clinton dull dull. All these guys except Clinton would've put Abbie to sleep.

Abbie would have been very unhappy with Clinton's sell-out on NAFTA and his failure of nerve on universal health care and his wimpy nowhereness on the environment and much more. But he'd've loved (and envied) those blow jobs in the White House. Oral sex in the oval office? YIPPIE!!!

Abbie would have driven the Dems to distraction and the Republicans to pure fury and revenge. In fact, Dave Dellinger left this world believing Abbie was murdered. Others believed the same of Marshall Bloom. Who's to say otherwise? What do we really know?

For thirty-five years now "Come, let us reason together" has been a losing line. Abbie's Chicago was the pivot. With the great Paul Krassner, with Dellinger and Jerry Rubin and Tom Hayden and a few other fellow incendiaries, he played media master, the political pied piper who drew a few thousand young marchers like me to see and make history.

When I finally met him in the early eighties, we had both moved on to the issue of the environment, especially nuclear power, the new Vietnam with a radioactive twist. Abbie, being Abbie, had run up an entire new life of incredible activism. As Barry Freed he assumed an entire new activist persona. Under a new name he brought his old skills to bear on such issues as saving the St. Lawrence River. In the 1980s, back above ground, back as Abbie, but grown still more, he put the CIA on trial, escorted young activists to Nicaragua to see the revolution as it happened, fought nuclear waste transport, worked to save the Delaware River, and helped form and served as the major advisor of a national Student Action Union to bring up a new generation on the issues of apartheid, tuition gouging, and more. Who but Abbie could just ramble through so many new personas without even batting an eye? Yippie!!!

As one would expect, our first visit was with his parole officer. From there we went to the tiny apartment he shared with his magnificent running mate, Johanna Lawrenson.

All the way, it was non-stop speed rap. The latest plans. The latest scams. Reagan was in the White House. Vietnam was a bad memory. The contras were on. Iraq was yet to come.

But hip and yip and revolution and the hell of it were at the core of Abbie's genetic code. And so were the more mundane commitments to social justice, political equality, a fair shake, and an honest opinion, about all of which he was supremely articulate.

But never boring. Never never never. That (along with paying retail) was the ultimate cardinal sin. And when are the liberals going to learn this?

Read *Hell of It* wrong and it'll seem like a relic, a cutesy reminder of a bygone age, when people still giggled about smoking pot. Better you should take a nap.

Because this book, like Abbie, is really a live volcano, a timeless testimony to the core commitments of someone smart enough to transform them into performance art for an electronic age. Chicago, the cops, the clubbings, the tear gas . . . they're all just props for a supremely aggressive intellect and a powerful heart deeply rooted in social justice issues that are timeless.

Abbie knew how to make it fun while taking the beatings, how to make it work while ignoring the faction fights, how to make it sexy while getting kicked.

Abbie! Abbie!! Abbie!!! Where the hell are you, now that we need you more than ever?

What you still do for us all in this genius of a book is to show how combining a relentless passion for peace and social justice with the joy of great writing, brilliant theater, and savvy organizing can work to change the world.

A revolution indeed.

But the real hell of it, dear brother, is how much we miss you.

—Harvey Wasserman
Bexley, Ohio
Winter 2005

Harvey Wasserman, a long-time friend and brother of Abbie Hoffman, is senior advisor to Greenpeace USA, senior editor of www.freepress.org, and author of Harvey Wasserman's History of the United States.

INTRODUCTION

This Spirit is among us now, refusing to sit for his portrait. He's in flight, with a toy gun, an ancient dare in his eye. No, Abbie's nothing like your average famous dead person. He has no time to waste—he's in a hurry! Take this book's title. One of the entendres you can find in all the comic hells spinning from the phrase "Revolution for the Hell of It" is a whimsical version of Crazy Horse's "Today is a good day to die." And with Abbie's jailed, on the lam, and dying-too-young life—we definitely remember him as reveling along the trajectory of carefree and at risk, and oh we miss it.

We know very well that we ourselves are now at risk, but we have reason to fear that we've lost FREE. Haven't seen it, not for a while. That flying abandon, the fun that makes Abbie's kind of "life-acting" possible. I can agree wholeheartedly when he argues that "the key to organizing an alternative society is to let peoples' abilities and desires evolve the ideology." Well, Abbie, we tried to do that, but something happened. Let me explain. You can replace that word *ideology* in your sentence with the word *sales* and you're looking at our generation's essential fork in the road.

Tracking desire, fun, YIPPIE!—and not spending that data as capital, but rather, calling it the key to social change? Wow. Let's talk plain here—there is no Abbie Hoffman now and there is no event with an edge that could frame him. A stage like the Republican National Convention in New York was supposed to have its radicalizing mimetic moment. I remember lots of people panting heavily while we painted our signs and arranged for lawyers in the supposedly hot summer of 2004. But this RNC was different than the 1968 Democratic Convention in Chicago in a way that we have yet to understand. We know deep down, though—FREE really must be here. After the poignancy of the February 15, 2003, peace march and after the unbelievable reelection of George Bush, after all our desperate theater, our puppets and chants and rants and signage, we have to wonder— where is FREE? Until FREE comes back, there will be no work- ers climbing the Winter Palace steps singing Mayakovsky, no standing in front of the Tiananmen tanks with a bouquet of flow- ers, no Mario Savio up on the tipping point of a police car launch- ing his Free Speech.

A fascinating part of this book is Abbie's acute study of the signs coming from power, and his often on-the-move or in-the- chaos invention of counter signs. What a Situationist Vaudevillian he was. Re: his blow-by-blow in Lincoln Park in the windy city— a careening multi-channel narrative in which he drives the action grandly and observes it minutely. You can't help but feel that he would have a solution to our current overwhelming agit-prop of war. For an obvious instance, what would he have to say about Bush's salute in pilot gear under the Mission Accomplished sign? You can sense Abbie locating the ironies. The same month that Bush walked across that aircraft carrier, SUVs were being sold on televised carrier decks between baseball innings. So the gas- burning consumer item that forces the war as much as anything does, is, in turn, sold by the same war. In this dizzying circularity, the meaning of heretofore immovably clear words such as *war* and *peace* are fuzzed, fogged, and finally switched. Yes—we sus- pect that Abbie would have already switched the words, just as he cast hell on this cover where you might have preferred something more like heaven. Karl Rove, with his *really* hellish alchemy of apocalypse and corporate marketing, never met the trickster he deserved.

YIP reader: experience this *Revolution for the Hell of It* as a nos- talgic event at your peril. Don't read it to remember getting laid, or to re-hum the music, or to sigh with a big flashback. That would mean that FREE accepted an acting job for a TV movie that adver- tises sweatshop sneakers in Vietnam. We can't let FREE do that. Yes, the sixties have been seized by counter-myths, just as the church owns the indigenous stories of Jesus. But we feel the force of those times like a wind that drives through our walls, through our traffic jams, through our neo-liberal lie. The sixties are always there, like the 1840s' utopian experiments that persisted till the Great War. Those days and nights of a half-century ago are a fine dust hanging between the molecules of culture, always imminent, becoming form again and appearing whole as an unmistakable personality, a song, a feeling of unexpected openness, the notion that an American war can be stopped. A friend named Carlo told me yesterday that the most popular movie last year among folks in their twenties was that story about Che Guevara, *The Motorcycle Diaries*. Really? FREE smiles.

Nowadays we can't seem to ask, "When's the Revolution?"—and why don't we? We're way back there with something more like "When do we have hope?" Come to think of it, how far apart are these two questions? Desperate hope and real change come hand in hand. In fact, have we forgotten that all change starts with three people at a table entertaining a notion? And there's probably some laughter in that talk.

Are we afraid that there is no consensus for social change, no reigning *Das Kapital*? How did Peace become expressed only as a grandiosity—hiding in history somewhere or frozen in a New Age painting? This book and this author-character Abbie Hoffman remind us that the wild self-discovering human has a causal relationship to august Peace. When I do suddenly feel hope, like I do after re-reading *Revolution for the Hell of It*, I feel the impossibility of a vacuum. I feel that all things impact all things; change is in the air because presiding human structures can be seen as operating by free choice, or anyway by the consensual hypnosis of the millions of consumers that still have freedom in them. When the social world looks like this electric pool, there can be a flash point so easily, and FREE rises for the perfect goof.

If Abbie refuses to be fetishized and isolated in historical time, he dares us to do the same. When I get his message, bravery isn't even a question. The ego of the Fool can suddenly prismatically refract across the beat of life, and Bushies (or your local corrupt Power) will bow before the change that comes from the crazy and the wise. It's the Spring solstice; it's Aquarius; it's the Clash singing the first notes of *London Calling*—it's all those things. It's the souls

of every revolutionary who spoke truth back at power and had the
spirit to move people to The Movement.

Abbie and his friends measured the Pentagon, paced it off. At
that moment it was already rising from the ground, turning sun-
orange, and flying off to general applause. We must ask ourselves, What is the thing that we do that releases Peace? It still
remains within us. How does the architecture of power become
no longer monumental, how do these deadly official policies lose
their skin of ads and show their absurdities? We have an emergency. People dying as I type. We have to start over now, and the
memory of Abbie Hoffman—and this is a lucky thing for us—
doesn't operate on us like another famous biography. He set it
up so that we remember him in the scary FREE moment of
direct political action.

One thing: If we jack ourselves to the new wonder, the bright lift
into Peace, the wake-up from Consumerism, we won't get there
imitating Abbie. Clearly if he were here now he wouldn't create
who he was then. Our discovery of social change is of our time, and
it's our responsibility. We just have to learn from the gift of his evo-
lutionary wild gene. And yes, it might begin by doing some personal things, like taking back the bursting rainbows of Abbie's time
from the product lines that stole them, retaking the colors for ourselves. When free expression crossed over to the tchotchkes and
we became listless in the aisles, FREE took the wrong drugs.

All Peace people are forced to start over now, and this book,
with its sophisticated rawness, is such an instruction manual for the
Peace we might need but don't yet recognize. And we won't get it
at all without laughing. There is a way in which we have become
sentimental without knowing it. My opinion? Somehow too many
laugh tracks changed our Yip! And don't we want to add some
Rabelais, some Groucho Marx and Sun Ra and Lenny Bruce and
Homer Simpson and Subcommandante Marcos and ACT UP and
Houdini and Bjork to our accustomed menu of Dr. King's letter
from jail and Gandhi's walk to the sea?

Abbie constantly tells us to get out the door and into the
adventure of public space. He walks out on St. Mark's Place with
that fierce funny openness and yes—he ignites a drama, breaks

down the inertia, people are flying away from him and toward him, staring, giggling, angry, shivering, relieved, laughing, and feeling sexy. That street is still there, and Peace is waiting for our mad FREE self.

Change-a-lujah!

—Bill Talen
aka Reverend Billy
Brooklyn, New York

Reverend Billy leads The Church of Stop Shopping, a group based in New York City that seeks to dramatically resist consumerism.

INTRODUCTION

Nov. 1, 1967

Dear Children,

When we were at Roberta's wedding on Oct. 29, Syd was there, and he asked us if we had seen last week's issue of *Time* magazine — we hadn't. So I went to the library on my lunch hour, and looked it up. This is what I found: "The N.Y. based National Mobilization Committee to End the War (alias MOB), the group that coordinated the march, headquartered in a *noisy Lower East Side Loft.* MOB is chaired by D. Dellinger, co-project director is wild-haired Jerry Rubin, an *uncompromising radical.* (Do you belong to this?) Others made it to Washington in MOB-organized car pools, etc. MOB also made money by selling high-camp posters. (Yours?)

"The *wildest plans, of course,* came from the *turned-on brains of the hippies.* 'Everybody knows that a 5-sided figure is evil,' said one N.Y. hippie named **FREE.** "The way to exorcise it is with a circle.' **FREE,** and a *hippie poster painter, Martin Carey,* last month 'measured' the Pentagon to determine how many hippies would be needed to encircle it (answer: 1200). The *oddly costumed pair was arrested for 'littering'* and hailed before a General Services Administrator." (What is that?) *Where is your self-respect? arrested?* "They asked for a permit to levitate the Pentagon 300 feet off the ground, explaining that by chanting ancient Aramaic exorcism rites while standing in a circle around the building, they could get it to rise into the air, turn orange, and vibrate until all evil emissions had fled. The war would end forthwith. The administrator graciously gave his permission for them to raise the building a maximum of 10 feet, and dismissed the charges against the hippies." (*Very nice!*)

"Fearful that forces would spray them with Mace, the hippies concocted a spray called LACE. Purportedly a purplish aphrodisiac brewed by the *flipped-out* pharmacist of hippiedom, A. O. Stanley III, Lace 'makes you want to take off your clothes, kiss people and make love.' Other hippie plots included jamming gun barrels with flowers, and an attempt to 'kidnap LBJ while wrestling him to the ground and *pulling his pants off!'* !!! 'We'll attack with noisemakers, water pistols, etc. Holy men will join hands and scream, 'Vote for me.' The light-hearted surrealism of the hippie approach was soon short-circuited by the hard-line elements. Hanoi was quick to capitalize on the latter's efforts."

Well, I'll tell you, that really topped it off! I used to think I had a sense of humor, but I surely don't think that was very funny! Of course you made light of it, saying it was "play-acting," but I think it was disgusting, and nauseating — especially the part about LBJ. I'm telling you, it made us feel *real* good! I am *thoroughly ashamed* to think my children had anything to do with it. I just hope that nobody else sees it. *What is getting into you?????*

Also (from an article written by a N.Y. *Times* writer for the paper), "Bare-chested hippies calling for mass fornication that night." Yes, I'm stupid, so I had to look it up, and when I found out what it meant, I couldn't believe it! How obscene and disgusting can they get?

I used to be so proud of all that you kids did, but now I just don't know. If you didn't have *such potential,* it would be different, but how can you waste what you have on such trash????? I can't understand it at all!

T. & C. were here last Saturday, and T. *insists* you all are *not* hippies and that you've stopped taking drugs. Now I don't know *what* to believe. If you are not hippies, how do you explain being grouped with them???

It is the *action of children,* not *supposedly grown, mature, intelligent adults.*

Aren't you ashamed *for your children? You* are acting like children! The more I think about it, the more I can't believe that any of you would be part of anything so *childish and stupid!*

There must have been something wrong in the way we

brought you up — I thought (or at least *we tried*) to bring you up to *respect law and order, other people's property, etc.* If I did anything like that, I would be ashamed for my children's sake, if not my own!

For months I was a nervous wreck (between T.'s draft status and the fact that I knew you were all taking drugs, etc. Now T. *assures me* you've stopped, and he is OK, as far as the draft) — so now *this* — I am constantly afraid to pick up the paper for fear I will see one of your names in it.

It seems it all started with your stupid jerk of a friend, **FREE**. (I can see you bristling.) I wake up at night, thinking about it, and *sweating*. You made it sound *so innocent* over the phone. You guys can be so convincing. According to you, all the papers and magazines are liars.

Believe me, I think if I didn't go to work, I'd go out of my mind!

You talk of moving to California. I don't know — maybe that's where the *real "kooks"* are! I don't know which is worse! The girls at work have been asking me, "Do you feel OK, you look so tired?" Is it any wonder? — I'd be ashamed to tell them what's on my mind! I just *pray* they haven't read *Time*.

It's really something for parents to live with! You want your children to grow up to be *respectful* people (*you try your best*), and it hurts! No wonder I get pains in my chest, and rashes all over. Well, I guess that's part of life!

I hope for the *sake* of your *beautiful children* (whom we never see) that you wake up *before it's too late!*

If you *have* to make *Time* why can't it be for *something decent???* I also hate to think of the D. Susskind show. (When will it be on?)

The old saying "Small children, small worries — big children, big worries" is so true! I only hope that *your children* will make you proud of them, as *I* had once hoped!

I had to *write* this, as I could never *say* it without breaking down, so here it is — I had to get it out of my system. You have such *potential* — maybe before we die, we'll see it realized!

All you do, usually, is laugh at what I say, but believe me, it's no laughing matter! You know it all!

In spite of it all, we love you — that's why we care so much what happens to you, and it hurts so much! You have children so you should know what I mean.

Now you talk of writing a book? I shudder to think about what will be in it?

We'll probably be ostracized (?) for this letter, but I don't care. OK — that's it, like it or not! I'm sorry but it had to be written.

Love,
MOM

1

REVOLUTION FOR THE HELL OF IT

REVOLUTION:
THE HIGHEST TRIP OF THEM ALL

"In a Revolution one wins or dies."
    — MAJOR ERNESTO "CHÉ" GUEVARA

"Dash: A revolution in cleansing powder."
    From a TV commercial

Revolution for the hell of it? Why not? It's all a bunch of phony words anyway. Once one has experienced LSD, existential revolution, fought the intellectual game-playing of the individual in society, of one's identity, one realizes that action is the only reality; not only reality but morality as well. One learns reality is a subjective experience. It exists in my head. I am the Revolution. The other day I took some LSD somewhere in the Florida Keys, where I've come to try to write a book. It's an interesting setting: exactly equidistant from Havana and Miami Beach. You are always reminded of the fact because Radio Havana is one of the clearest radio stations. They play terrible crap music and you wonder why they don't play Country Joe and the Fish or the Beatles. That would be good propaganda. It seems as if they are trying to convert all the retirees who waddle around in Bermuda shorts. You wonder what they have in mind. Anyway, all of a sudden a tropical storm hit and the sky turned black. I thought (felt) it was a tornado and before I knew it the house had become unfastened and was spinning wildly in the air like a scene from *The Wizard of Oz*. Paul Krassner, who was watching television, shouted that Stokely had just returned and had been grabbed by the FBI. Everybody

is hallucinating a mile a minute. "Shit, Tim Leary, I'm sorry I
said LSD was a fake." I'm laughing away, dreaming of the
house getting blown to Cuba with the floor shaking like a
son-of-a-bitch. "The Revolution Is On!" I scream and grab a
cap pistol, preparing to shoot the first cop that comes along.
My wife joins in the game and we have this whole *Bonnie and
Clyde* thing going. It's all hilarious, really. One big revolution
for the hell of it. The point is, if it were a real gun and a cop
walked in, I would have shot him dead. BANG! What are the
guidelines for revolution when the house has been cast adrift
in a tornado? What of the debates between Marat and Sade
when the inmates run wild? Listen to Fidel Castro:

There are those who believe that it is necessary for ideas to
triumph among the greater part of the masses before initiating
action, and there are others who understand that action is one
of the most efficient instruments for bringing about the triumph
of ideas among the masses. Whoever hesitates while waiting
for ideas to triumph among the masses before initiating revolutionary action will never be a revolutionary. Humanity will,
of course, change; human society will, of course, continue to
develop — in spite of men and the errors of men. But that is
not a revolutionary attitude.
   *(Speech delivered by Major Fidel Castro Ruiz at the clos-
   ing of the First Conference of the Latin American Organization of Solidarity (OLAS), August 10, 1967.)*

THERE IS NO WAY
TO RUN A REVOLUTION

Revolution is in your head. You are the Revolution.
Do your thing
Do your thing
Do your thing

Do your thing
Do your thing
Be your thing
Practice. Rehearsals come after the act. Act. Act. One practices
by acting. Billy the Kid strides with 6 guns blazing, receding
into his inner space. What does he find? Another Billy the Kid
striding with 6 guns blazing, receding into his inner space.
There are no rules, only images. Only a System has boundaries.
Eichmann lives by the rules. Eichmann, machinelike, twitching
nervously, pushes at his steel-rimmed glasses, takes his neatly
folded handkerchief from the breast pocket of his gray-flannel
suit and mops his sweating bald forehead (AN ELECTRICAL EN-
GINEER: *"My goal in life is to make myself replaceable"* — DOT–
DOT–BEEP–BEEP).

"My God was a pink memo. Uh . . ." he stutters, "excuse me,
my God was a pink memo on Tuesdays, on Wednesdays it was
a blue memo. . . . It's hard to remember exactly. Yes, yes, that
was it. Pink memo on Tuesdays, blue memo on Wednesdays."

Eichmann lets out a huge sigh of relief, smiles a little pince-
nez smile, carefully refolds his handkerchief and replaces it in
his pocket.

"I was a careerist. (s l o w) I   was   only   doing   my   death."

Behind Billy the Kid stands Abraham. Grand old man of
9,000 years, striding across the desert lands, sweat crushed
against his brow by a huge sun-baked forearm of golden fleece,
the same golden fleece that hung from his head and face in
cascading waves of hard times.

God says, "Abraham, take your beloved son Isaac to the
land of Moriah and place him upon an altar and make of him
a sacrifice."

And Abraham tightens his fists and gnarls his teeth and cries
out, "How do I know that is the God that has guided me and
my people all these years?"

Inside he knows because He is God, which is to say, a Man
and not a machine. He bids goodbye to Sarah, whom he truly

loves, and he walks, holding his young son's tender hand, the three miles to Moriah. Placing his son upon the carefully constructed altar, he binds and gags him to let his son know that he loves him, and yet he does not need to do that because the boy too loves his father and needs no bindings. There would be no pain. Then Abraham dabs the boy with holy water that he had carried from his holy well and recites a few ritual prayers, mumbling them rotely because three days ago when he talked to God, he had already decided he would do what he must do. He holds his left hand over his son's eyes and raises the long well-used knife in the air, poising it for that final plunge. One plunge, quickly, for the steel in his mighty arm—sword will need but one thrust upon the young lad's frail body.

"Abraham, I am your God."

He slumps, exhausted with joy. It was an orgasm of consciousness, pulsating down rows upon rows of mankind.

Trust your impulses. Trust your impulses. TRUST – TRUST – TRUST – TRUST – TRUST – TRUST – TRUST TRUST – TRUST – TRUST – TRUST
   Test
     Test
       Test
         Relax

The trouble with liberalism and bull-shit American middle class DOT–DOT–BEEP–BEEPs is that they run the myth backwards.

"God is dead," they cry, "and we did it for the kids."

A true revolutionist carves the revolution out of Granite Rock. Ho Chi Minh crawls through the Mekong Delta rice-paddy mud and comes to a fork in the road. A road, by the way, that he and he alone constructed. Environment is in your head. Your head is a granite rock of neural impulses, get some dynamite if you need it.

Billy the Kid blazes his motorcycle down that neural impulse road and thrashes madly, gears lock, guns fall from his side in the jolt, the chrome-plated Harley-Davidson rears on its hind legs. Oop! He sails from the sturdy bike, hurled into inner space.

People said he was such a nice young kid.

"Why, I remember the time young Billy used to like to run naked from the swimmin' hole down through town, still dripping wet."

Not exactly Lady Godiva, I'll admit. Billy sure was a hot shit in those days.

"Can't figger him out now, he must have flipped."

Yeah, sure, that was it, he must have flipped out. Crazy motherfucker Billy.

"Billy come back, come back, Billy, Billy, Billy."

Go Billy! Go! Go! Billy Go. We don't need leaders. We need cheerleaders. Go Billy Go!! Do your thing! Sock it to 'em!

Fidel sits on the side of a tank rumbling into Havana on New Year's day. His green army fatigues swiped from Batista's Free Store, sent down by John Foster Dulles, who, adding a touch of creativity to his cousin Eichmann's idea, decided that if everyone in Latin America wore American Army fatigues, all the problems would be solved. Clever Yankee was John Foster Dulles. Fidel's rifle lies like a feather cradled in his strong arms. Girls throw flowers at the tank and rush to tug playfully at his black beard. He laughs joyously and pinches a few rumps, for he is a soldier and they like to do that sort of thing, you know. The tank stops in the city square. Fidel lets the gun drop to the ground, slaps his thighs and stands erect. He is like a mighty penis coming to life, and when he is tall and straight, the crowd immediately is transformed.

"Now the Revolution begins."

He goes to a friend's house, collapses on the floor, snoring loudly, exhausted from five days without sleep, and sleeps for twenty straight hours.

For ten long years he builds a country. Makes love. Steals Russian rubles. Sticks a finger in Uncle Sam's nose.

"We are going to do away with money, people should relate to each other as human beings."

Go Fidel Go! Go Fidel Go! Go Fidel Go! Do your thing! Sock it to 'em!

He fires Commie Dean Ruskies who say he is going mad (not publicly of course) and makes the revolution.

This Byzantine discussion about the ways and means of struggle, whether it should be peaceful or non-peaceful, armed or unarmed — the essence of this discussion, which we call Byzantine because it is like an argument between two deaf and dumb people, is what distinguishes those who want to promote revolution and those who do not want to promote it. Let no one be fooled.*

And again he "meditates" like Siddhartha sitting cross-legged under the flower-blossomed Bo tree . . .

These years have taught us all to meditate more and analyze better. We no longer accept any "self-evident" truths. "Self-evident" truths belong to bourgeois philosophy. A whole series of old clichés must be abolished. Marxist literature itself, revolutionary political literature itself, should be renewed because repeating the same old clichés, phraseology and verbiage that have been repeated for 35 years wins over no one, convinces no one at all. There are times when political documents, called Marxist, give the impression that someone has gone to an archive and asked for a form: form 14, form 13, form 12; they are all alike, with the same empty words, in language incapable of expressing real situations. Very often, these documents are divorced from real life. And then many people are told that this is Marxism . . . and in what way is this different from a catechism. and in what way is it different from a litany, from a rosary?**

And finally, shooting down communism, Christianityism, Lyndon Baines Johnsonism, Old Ageism, he says,

* Castro speech at closing of OLAS conference, Aug. 10, 1967.
** Ibid.

The communist movement developed a method, a style, and in some aspects, even took on the characteristics of a religion. And we sincerely believe that the character should be left behind. Of course, to some of these "illustrious revolutionary thinkers" we are only petit bourgeois adventurers without revolutionary maturity. We are lucky that the Revolution came before maturity!*

All this while still sitting cross-legged under the flower-blossomed Bo tree in the center of Havana.

*   *   *   *

AN EXPLANATION

What does free speech mean to you? To me it is an image like all things.
ME: Yes, I believe in total free speech.
INTERVIEWER: Well, surely you don't believe in the right
                           to cry "fire" in a crowded theatre?
ME: F I R E !

Conversation with the Reader

What goes through your head when you read this pudding? Images? Images of who? Me? You? I am a myth. Besides I can't write and words are all bullshit anyway. I don't know how to write. Here is an example of what I mean. It is called a poem. I didn't call it that, someone else did. I called it a brown manila envelope. It is a manila envelope about meetings. It was fun to write.

* Ibid.

DIGGER CREED FOR HEAD MEETINGS
MEETINGS ARE
INFORMATION
MEDITATION
EXPERIENCE
FUN
TRUST
REHEARSALS
DRAMA
HORSESHIT
MEETINGS ARE NOT
PUTTING PEOPLE DOWN
Shhhh!   LISTEN AT MEETINGS   Shhhhhh!
LISTEN TO eye movements
LISTEN TO scratching
LISTEN TO your head
LISTEN TO smells
LISTEN TO singing
LISTEN TO touches
LISTEN TO silence
LISTEN TO gestalt vibrations
LISTEN TO a baby born in the sea
LISTEN TO the writing on the wall
DON'T LISTEN TO WORDS
DON'T LISTEN TO WORDS
DON'T LISTEN TO WORDS
meetings are life
surrender to the meeting . . . the meeting is the message
MEETINGS ARE CONFRONTATION —
MEETINGS ARE RELAXATION —
DIG OTHER HEADS —
DIG YOUR HEAD
dig disrupters, dig poets, dig peacemakers, dig heads who
mumble, dig heads who don't go to meetings, dig heads
who fall asleep, dig andy kent, dig clowns, dig street fight-

ers, dig heads who scribble on paper, dig hustlers, dig
heads that admit they are wrong, dig heads that know they
are right, dig doing, dig changes, dig holy men, DIG HEADS
who do everything
AT MEETINGS DIG HEADS WHO DIG MEETINGS
all meetings are the same same same same same same
same same same same same same same — DIFFERENT
meetings are rivers   —   don't build dams

    BEWARE OF STRUCTURE FREAKS
    BEWARE OF RULES
    BEWARE OF "AT THE LAST MEETING WE
        DECIDED . . ."
DON'T GO BACK — THERE WAS NO LAST MEETING
DON'T GO FORWARD — THERE IS NOTHING
meetings are Now   you are the meeting   we are Now
WITHOUT MEETINGS THERE IS NO COMMUNITY
        COMMUNITY IS UNITY
AVOID GANGBANGS ...   RAPE IDEAS NOT PEOPLE
        MAKE LOVE AT ALL MEETINGS
MEETINGS TAKE A MOMENT — Time is Fantasy —
MEETINGS TAKE FOREVER
        there is no WAY to run a meeting
use meetings to help you DO YOUR THING
Go naked to meetings   —   Go high to meetings
        BE PREPARED
PREPARE BY meditation
PREPARE BY doing
COME PREPARED TO DROP OUT   —   COME PRE-
PARED TO STAY FOREVER
IF YOU ARE NOT PREPARED MEETINGS ARE NOT YOUR
THING
        ONLY DO YOUR THING
    mene, mene, tekel, upharsin

        (meetings are a pain in the ass)

Once about three months ago, or four or five, I got a call that there was "trouble" on the streets. There was a knock on the door and a nervous young kid whom I like stammered out things like "Ninth Precinct" and "arrests." I got dressed in my cowboy clothes and walked three blocks down to the Ninth Precinct. The night air was chilly. It was Saturday night and the streets were teeming with the run-of-the-mill chaos. Paul, Anita, Barry, Phyllis, and I strode along. I was headed for a revolutionary encounter. "Here we all go to the Ninth Pre-cinct, Ninth Precinct, Ninth Precinct." When we finally reached the station house entrance all sorts of information was flying around the air. We had come on some issue regarding a rock band called Salvation that had got busted for something or other, or so Barry said and Captain Fink concurred.

Captain Fink and I are old friends. "Friends," I had said to him, "ain't got nothing to do with it. Some of my best friends are enemies." He has a copy of a poem I wrote. He confessed to me he didn't understand Allen Ginsberg. Captain Fink is Jewish sometimes, just like me. Once I said to him what my relatives always said to me: "What's a nice Jewish guy like you doing in a place like this." I like to talk Yiddish in front of him, especially if there are goy cops in hearing distance, He doesn't understand Yiddish. I speak only a few lines, but he thinks I'm a Talmudic scholar. It's a funny little game. This time, how-ever, I am here on "business."

The fact that Fink is here on Saturday night is heavy infor-mation. Other information is flying around the air. Lots of black people are running back and forth. I'm very interested in this because I'm trying to build links with people outside the sys-tem. I guess it's called being an organizer or a missing link. It seems, upon talking to a group of very young black kids, that 20 or so of their friends have just been arrested in a large pot bust. This is what I call bad news/good news.

BAD NEWS: Cops bust black people;
hippies won't get busted when they
smoke pot in large groups because of

racism (hippies in strange way better
organized than blacks in the power politics pressure game on the Lower East
Side); blacks will be pissed at hippies.
*Cops manipulate intergroup frictions
through politics.*

GOOD NEWS: I'm there and there is a
chance to play missing link, to join
forces with blacks. I have a stage.

While everybody is shaking their heads and advising and
huddling and yelling, I lie down in front of the station-house
door. Nobody can get out of the police station. People, cops,
spades, Captain Fink are all confused.

Phyllis yells, "He's been stabbed!"

A tug of war develops between us and them, with me as the
rope. I'm in meditation, just lying there smiling while the
cops drag me into the station house. Fink confronts me.

"FREE, this isn't your business. They aren't hippies. Why
don't you go home."

"What do you mean, 'hippie'? I'm a nigger and I was smoking pot with them. Arrest me or let them go."

The cops put me in the back room. I'm jiving with the
spades. I bum a cigarette from one. We're all brothers. Most
think I'm crazy, same as Fink and the cops, but one little kid
they picked up, he must have been twelve years old, is smiling
and winking. You know the smile I mean? Fink comes in and
tries again to get me to go home. I tell him I'm just doing my
job and he'd better place me under arrest before I burn down
the police station. He walks out of the room, sweating. I'm getting restless.

"What is this bullshit. Am I under arrest or not. Asshole
cops, you don't know your job." I follow Fink into the main
lobby of the station. Everybody's farting around.

"Am I under arrest or not?" I shout. Nobody answers.

I raise my cowboy boot and kick in Captain Fink's trophy

case window. The glass flies all over the place and Fink, turning red in the face (he seemed to be losing his temper for some reason), shouts, "You're under arrest."

"It's about fuckin' time," I respond. Even the cops are laughing at the "Ol' Man," as they call him.

I'm led away and booked. The rest is anticlimax. A night in the Tombs. Court scene. Judge: "Do you realize that this leads to anarchy?" (That's as good a word as any, so I smile.)

People have asked me why I did what I did at the station house and I told them a story similar to the one I just told here, but it was all bullshit. I really did it because it was fun. That's what I tell my friends. To my brothers I tell the real truth, which is that I don't know why I did it. They smile because they know any explanation I give is made up.

2

THE RISING OF THE PENTAGON

Spring is here and things are popping. On Easter Sunday there was a huge Be-In in Central Park. There were probably 30,000 people that Was-In. It was hard to tell — it was all over the place. Everybody high on something: balloons, acid, bananas, kids, sky, flowers, dancing, kissing. I had a ball — totally zonked. People kept giving away things free — fruit, jelly beans, clothes, flowers, chicken, Easter eggs, poems. Leaving the park, I strolled down Fifth Avenue singing "In your Easter bonnet . . ." and every once in a while yelling "Draft Cardinal Spellman." All of a sudden there it was, St. Patrick's Cathedral, a huge gray mouldering bastion, loudspeakers urging "Come on in." I'm very calm now, cross the street when it says WALK, mount the steps and then — "Hey, you, buddy!" A line of cops wiggling their index fingers. "You can't go in with that uniform" (flowers, gold paint, Easter bunny).

"Why not, officer? You can go in with yours."

"You can't go in the church with flowers in your hair. It's the Cardinal's orders."

"It's my Easter suit — I want to go in the church." Assume the stance. Crowd gathers. Have to work tonight, Freedom, goals, what's important . . . Silence . . . Staring . . . "Keep your damn church, we got the park anyway." Angry at self later — chickened out — who knows . . . There's time to get them later.

March 30, 1967

THE
CHARGE
OF THE
FLOWER
BRIGADE

There we sat in a corner of Central Park going through all the changes that you go through before direct action. Sixteen members of the Flower Brigade preparing to march in the Support Our Boys in Vietnam parade. "Shit, I'm scared. I almost didn't make it up on the subway," says one kid. Joe Flaherty of the *Village Voice* drops by to tell us it's like walking into the lion's den. Jim Fouratt says he's definitely marching. He called the parade committee and was assured we were an officially designated group in the parade and he has this marvelous cherub look that says "we got to show them our love." The *Daily News* reporter comes by: "Where are all your members?"

"They went AWOL," someone quips. "If Jim goes I guess we all go." No one cops out. Since I'm supposed to know about this stuff I do my OK-I-think-we're-gonna-get-the-shit-kicked-out-of-us speech. It's a quickie on non-violent defense, about removing earrings, protecting genitals and base of the head, staying together as a group, etc. Jim talks to the cops. They are going to escort us to Lexington and 93rd, our assembly point. They try to talk us out of going. Some cop's on a walkie-talkie and orders are that we get no escort. Just then a patrol car rides by with a "Support Our Boys" sticker on the windshield.

We figure it's safer without the cops. Off come as many identifying items as possible. All we got are flowers. We march the five blocks without incident and form behind a Boy Scout group from Queens. It's sunny and we're really grooving. Glad there's no trouble, we wait for about an hour. Some bystanders who like what we're doing buy us more flowers to carry. We all have American flags, some guys have official Support Our Boys banners that they bought from vendors who came by. I have a beautifully colored cape that says FREEDOM all over it. Anita is dressed in red, white and blue. Three people have pink posters that say "Love" on them. A few college hawkniks come by. One guy swings, wants to get laid, takes a flower and says he'll even march with us. The Boy Scouts are really digging us goofing around: "Hey, they're kissing, look at that."

The Scout leaders are having a real time controlling the kids. They make them line up with their right arms extended two inches below Heil Hitler position. They order them to face front. Everything looks cool. We're all impatient to get going. The word goes out: "We're movin' out." OK. "Left, Right, Left, Right, Left, Right" or "Right, Left." The Boy Scouts are really showing us up. We march a half block to Park Avenue. You can really hear the bands now. It's John Philip Sousa Day in Fun City. Man, I dig parades. A busty mother walks by with her four-year-old twins dressed in Army clothes, each with a plastic machine gun. Two Bircher type women see us. They ask the cops what's going on. The cop shrugs his shoulders. They confer with the Boy Scout leaders.

They decide that we are a corrupting influence. They march the Scouts around the Flatbush Conservative Club contingent. We follow. We get cut off from the Boy Scouts. "Be Prepared!" Zonk! Fists, red paint, kicks, beer cans, spitting — the whole American Welcome Wagon treatment. They grab our American flags and rip them up. Quite an interesting bit, since this parade was formed chiefly because of the flag-burning at the April 15 peace march. Daisy petals flying all over like chicken feathers. A mother drops her baby in order to get in a few well-placed kick punches. The baby's getting crushed along with the flower people. The baby's one of us, while Mom does her patriotic thing. Two girls are stomped on. We sound the retreat. "Get those bearded creeps!" (No one had a beard.) "Cowards! Cowards!" "Go back to the Village!" Cops appear out of nowhere. There is a flying wedge. We are marched to Second Avenue and get a police escort to St. Marks Place.

The Flower Brigade lost its first battle, but watch out, America. We were poorly equipped with flowers from uptown florists. Already there is talk of growing our own. Plans are being made to mine the East River with daffodils. Dandelion chains are being wrapped around induction centers. Holes are being dug in street pavements with seeds dropped in and covered. The cry of "Flower Power" echoes through the land. We shall not wilt. Let a thousand flowers bloom.

April 29, 1967

SKULLDIGGERY

This Digger phenomenon deserves a close examination by the peace movement — not that these jottings will necessarily make things clearer; clarity, alas, is not one of our goals. Confusion is mightier than the sword!

First it is important to distinguish between hippies and Diggers. Both are myths: that is, there is no definition, there is no organized conspiracy; both are in one sense a huge put-on. Hippies, however, are a myth created by media and as such they are forced to play certain media-oriented roles. They are media-manipulated. Diggers too are myth, but a grass-roots myth created from within. We have learned to manipulate media. Diggers are more politically oriented but at the same time bigger fuckoffs. Diggers are zenlike in that we have totally destroyed words and replaced them with "doing" — action becomes the only reality. Like Lao-tzu: *"The way to do is to be."* We cry, "No one understands us," while at the same time, winking out of the corner of our eye, recognizing that if the straight world understood all this Digger shit, it would render us impotent, because understanding is the first step to control and control is the secret to our extinction.

This reluctance to define ourselves gives us glorious freedom in which to fuck with the system. We become communist-racist-acid-headed freaks, holding flowers in one hand and bombs in the other. The Old Left says we work for the CIA. Ex-Marines stomp on us as Pinkos. Newport police jail us as smut peddlers. Newark cops arrest us as riot inciters. (These four events were all triggered by passing out free copies of the same poem.) So what the hell are we doing, you ask? We are dynamiting brain cells. We are putting people through changes. The key to the puzzle lies in theater. We are theater in the streets: total and committed. We aim to involve people and use (unlike other movements locked in ideology) any weapon (prop) we can find. The aim is not to earn the respect, admiration, and love of everybody — it's to get people to do, to participate, whether positively or negatively. All is relevant, only "the play's the thing."

. . . Stand on a street corner with 500 leaflets and explode. Give some to a sad-looking female. Tell guys that pass, "Hey, can you help her out? She can't do it by herself and her father's a communist cell leader and will beat her up if she doesn't pass them out." Recruit a person to read the leaflet aloud while all this distribution is going on. Run around tearing the leaflets, selling them, trading them. Rip one in half and give half to one person and half to another and tell them to make love. Do it all fast. Like slapstick movies. Make sure everyone has a good time. People love to laugh — it's a riot. Riot — that's an interesting word-game if you want to play it.

Don't be for or against. Riots — environmental and psychological — are Holy, so don't screw around with explanations. Theater also has some advantages. It is involving for those people that are ready for it while at the same time dismissed as nonthreatening by those that could potentially wreck the stage. It's dynamite. By allowing all: loving, cheating, anger, violence, stealing, trading, you become situation-oriented and as such become more effective. You believe in participatory democracy (especially when talking to a New Left audience), only you call it "everyone doing his thing." You let people decide, no strings attached. During the riots in Newark we smuggled in food, giving it to our underground soul brothers SNCC and NCUP (Newark Community Union Project).

"We brought a lot of canned goods, Tom, so the people can eat them or throw them at the cops."

Like many of the people in the riot, we dug the scene. Had a ball passing out food. Seven truckloads in all. And that's another key to the riddle: Dig what you're doing! Make war on paranoia. Don't be afraid. Don't get uptight. There's a war against property going on. I ask an old black woman in Newark, "What's going on?" and she tells me they stole her shoes and she's roaring with laughter. Spades and Diggers are one. Diggersareniggers. Both stand for the destruction of property. There are many ways to destroy property: to change is to destroy — give it away free. The free thing (another clue) is the most revolutionary thing in America today. Free dances, free food, free theater (constantly), free stores, free bus rides, free dope, free housing, and most important, free money. Theater will capture the attention of the country, the destruction of the monetary system will bring it to its knees. Really fuck with money. Burn it, smoke it to get high, trade with it, set up boxes of it in the streets marked "Free Money," panhandle it, steal it, throw it away.

Scene: Washington Square Park. Actors: one very nicely dressed white liberal, one down-and-out-looking Digger. Audience: a large crowd of similar liberals, of various sexes. The title of the play: FOOD FOR NEWARK SPADES.

DIG.:   Sir, could you please spare a dollar for some food for Negroes in Newark?

LIB.:   Gee, I'm sorry, I don't have much money on me.

DIG: (still pleading, hat in hand) We're collecting food at

Liberty House.* Couldn't you buy a dollar's worth and
bring it over?

LIB.:   If I had a dollar, I certainly would.

DIG.:   (exploding) I think you're full of shit. Here's ten dollars (pulling out real American money and shoving it in
his face), go buy some food and bring it over to Liberty
House.

LIB.:   (getting a bit annoyed but still wanting to be polite)
Oh no, I couldn't take money from you.

DIG.:   (throwing the money on the ground) Well, there it is
on the ground, do something with it.

The Digger walks away dropping clues to understanding the
street drama: Liberty House, Black, Newark, Food, Free,
Money.

The rumors begin to fly as rumors always do. Rumors have
power. Like myths, people become involved in them, adding,
subtracting, multiplying. Get them involved. Let them participate. If it's spelled out to the letter there is no room for participation. Nobody participates in ideology. Never lie — Diggers
never lie. Once committed in a street drama, never turn back.
Be prepared to die if it's necessary to gain your point.

!   · !   !   !   !   !   !   !   !

Don't rely on words. Words are the absolute in horseshit.
Rely on doing — go all the way every time. Move fast. If you

* Liberty House is what first brought me to New York. It was set up
in the West Village to serve as a retail outlet for crafts made in cooperatives in Mississippi. It was a branch of the SNCC operations; some
of us under the leadership of Jesse Morris formed the Poor People's
Corporation and quickly trained poor blacks in craft skills and business management. We were told by all sorts of fancy economic experts that it was impossible to train these people, never mind giving
them control of the businesses. The experts might be interested in
knowing that the program not only has survived three years but has
expanded quite successfully without help from the government and
in an extremely hostile environment (Mississippi). This type of program is next best to FREE and we are developing a similar one for
the Lower East Side. If readers want to order catalogues of the products, they should write to Liberty House, 313 West Pascagoula
Street, Jackson, Miss.

spend too long on one play, it becomes boring to you and the audience. When they get bored, they are turned off. They are not receiving information. Get their attention, leave a few clues and vanish. Change your costume, use the props around you. Each morning begin naked. Destroy your name, become unlisted, go underground. Find brothers. Soul brothers. Black people, Puerto Ricans, Dropouts, Bowery Bums. Find out where they're at. Don't fuck with their thing. P.R.s dig manhood, don't play sissy. Black people dig pot, don't give them acid. Dropouts dig flowers, don't give them I. F. Stone weeklies. Bowery bums dig wine, don't give them Bibles. Become aware of the most effective props. On the Lower East Side pot is an effective prop, it is the least common denominator. It makes us all outlaws, brothers, niggers. Smoke it in public. It really has an effect on P.R.s, really challenges their concept of courage.

"Hey man, you're brave enough to kill someone, and not brave enough to smoke pot in the park!"

That kind of thing is a good deal more effective than sermons on the holiness of passive resistance. Use non-verbal props and media. Music is another denominator. Conga-Rock, get together. The Diggers and Pee Wee's gang (largest P.R. gang on New York's Lower East Side) threw a large dance at the Cheetah, a discotheque, on August 15. *Conga-Rock. Something for everybody. Do your thing. Don't give speeches. Don't have meetings. Don't have panel shows. They are all dead. Drama is anything you can get away with.* Remember that last peace demonstration? Do you recall the speeches or the Bread and Puppet Theater and Stokely yelling "Hell no, we won't go!" That was drama, not explanation. The point is nobody gives a shit anymore about troop strength, escalation, crying over napalm. A peace rally speech to me is like reading the *National Guardian* which is like watching the TV reports on Highway Fatalities which is like praying for riots to end which is like BULLSHIT! Herbert Marcuse says flower children have the answer. He smoked hashish at the big world happening in London in early August. Pray tell, what is a good Marxist to do?

Accept contradictions, that's what life is all about. Have a good time. Scrawled on the wall of the American pavilion at Expo '67 is our slogan in bright Day-glo: "It is the duty of all revolutionists to make love." Do weird things. Silly-putty sabotage and monkey warfare. John Roche, who is now intellectual-in-residence fink at the White House, once said that if Hitler had been captured in 1937, brought to Trafalgar Square, and had his pants pulled down, he could never have risen to power. Every time he tried one of those spectacular speeches the people would have just laughed at him because the image of "Mein Fuhrer" with his pants down around his ankles would have been too much.

Think about it.

PROPERTY is THEFT

PROPERTY is ROBBERY

(Choose one of the three —
choose the one that rhymes)

DRIVING
THE MONEY
CHANGERS
FROM THE
TEMPLE

At first I thought throwing out money at the Stock Exchange was just a minor bit of theater. I had more important things to do, like raising bail money for a busted brother. Reluctantly, I called up and made arrangements for a tour under the name of George Metesky, Chairman of East Side Service Organization (ESSO). We didn't even bother to call the press. About eighteen of us showed up. When we went in the guards immediately confronted us. "You are hippies here to have a demonstration and we cannot allow that in the Stock Exchange." "Who's a hippie? I'm Jewish and besides we don't do demonstrations, see we have no picket signs," I shot back. The guards decided it was not a good idea to keep a Jew out of the Stock Exchange, so they agreed we could go in. We stood in line with all the other tourists, exchanging stories. When the line moved around the corner, we saw more newsmen than I've ever seen in such a small area. We started clowning. Eating money, kissing and hugging, and that sort of stuff. The newsmen were told by the guards that they could not enter the gallery with us. We were ushered in and immediately started throwing money over the railing. The big tickertape stopped and the brokers let out a mighty cheer. The guards started pushing us and the brokers booed. When we got out, I carried on in front of the press.

"Who are you?"

"I'm Cardinal Spellman."

"Where did you get the money?"

"I'm Cardinal Spellman, you don't ask me where I get my money."

"How much did you throw out?"

"A thousand dollars in small bills."

"How many of you are there?"

"Two, three, we don't even exist! We don't even exist!"

We danced in front of the Stock Exchange, celebrating the end of money. I burned a fiver. Some guy said it was disgusting and I agreed with him, calling my comrades "Filthy Commies."

The TV show that night was fantastic. It went all over the world. TV news shows always have a pattern. First the "serious" news, all made up, of course, a few commercials, often constructed better than the news, then the Stock Market Report. Then the upswing human interest story to keep everybody happy as cows. Our thing came after the Stock Market Report, it was a natural. CBS, which is the most creative network, left in references to Cardinal Spellman; I was surprised at that. Every news report differed. Some said we threw out monopoly money, some said twenty–thirty dollars, some said over $100, some said the bills were all ripped up first. It was a perfect mythical event, since every reporter, not being allowed to actually witness the scene, had to make up his own fantasy. Some had interesting fantasies, some boring. One tourist who joined the exorcism got the point: "I'm from Missouri and I've been throwing away money in New York for five days now. This is sure a hell of a lot quicker and more fun."

May 20, 1967

4.

TRIP TO DENTON AND THE DIGGERS

Last week we went to a New Left–Old Left Conference in Denton, Michigan: Paul Krassner, Jim Fouratt, Keith Lampe,

Bob O'Keene and I. We were met by San Francisco Diggers Emmett Grogan, Peter Berg, Billy Tumbleweed, and a beautiful cat who just played a tamborine and smiled. It was a monumental meeting, probably never to be repeated. Jim and I were the only outwardly identifiable hippies from New York. Jim in his beautiful Goldilocks hair and purple pants, I in beads, boots, bellbottoms, and a cocky Mexican cowboy hat. Sitting in the Kalamazoo airport you sense the vibrations. Hippies are the new minority group. Diggersareniggers. I'm getting to understand what a black person goes through on a level not even reached by getting kicked around in the civil rights movement for four years. Anita and I were in Times Square the other night in costume. We panhandled a few cigarettes, which is really a gas. Panhandling really blows the mind when it's carried on by middle class drop-outs. A little guy full of *Daily News* bitterness shakes his fist at me. "You fuckin' coward, won't defend our country, won't go and fight, you cocksucker." I didn't even have one teeny-weeny peace button. He knew. The sides are drawn. When you meet another hippie in the street, especially outside the Village, you smile and say hello — a kind of comradeship that I've seen black people show when they are alone in the white world.

Back to the meeting: As we entered you could sense the vibrations as very mixed. You just have to walk around freaky-looking and you can tell where people's heads are. Tom Hayden was speaking. He was talking of the hard decision that faced NCUP over whether or not to join the poverty program in Newark. He carefully outlined the pros and cons and said that in the end there was no correct answer, there was no ideology you could turn to for reference. Then in came the Diggers. Tom is finished and all hell breaks out. We are hugging the Diggers. Grogan's yelling "One of us is in the can, is there a fuckin' lawyer here? What the hell you faggots looking at, get off your asses, we need help." They grab some fat cat who identifies himself as a lawyer and go off to the local pokey to bail out fellow Digger. Peter Berg, ex-San Francisco

Mime Trouper, founder of the Digger Free Store, "Trip Without a Ticket," starts to talk. He looks like a young angry Sitting Bull, only different . . . unique, a white Snick nigger. Rambling on — wow! It's pouring out like honey and vinegar, all mixed up. Scatalogical.° He's on a trip! Holy Shit. Excitement, Drama, Revolution. The message: Property is the enemy — burn it, destroy it, give it away. Don't let them make a machine out of you, get out of the system, do your thing. Don't organize students, teachers, Negroes, organize your head. Find out where you are, what you want to do and go out and do it. Johnson's a commie, the Kremlin is more fucked up than Alabama. Get out. Don't organize the schools, burn them. Leave them, they will rot. . . . The kids are getting stoned. We're all talking now. Lots of resistance. Kid says to me, "I like what you're saying and I'm going to drop out in a year." "What the hell you waiting for?" "Well, I want to finish school first." Reminded me of an SDS picket line I saw on a campus last year, protesting the tests used to determine draft status. Most of the demonstrators put their signs down and went in to take the test. These are the potential revolutionists? *Eich meir* a revolution!

Grogan re-enters, reconvenes the meeting single-handed. He climbs up on the table. Starts slow, sucks everyone in by answering a few questions. I'm sitting next to him, sleepy from sitting on my ass in Kalamazoo. All of a sudden he erupts and kicks the fuckin' table over. He knocks down a girl, slapping SDS'ers right and left. "Faggots! Fags! Take off your ties, they are chains around your necks. You haven't got the balls to go mad. You're gonna make a revolution? — you'll piss in your pants when the violence erupts. You, spade — you're a nigger, what are you doing here? Your people need you. There's a war on. They got fuckin' concentration camps ready, the world's going to end any day. Shut up and listen, I'll read a poem,

° It's funny — I'd always thought that word meant "in small pieces" like "scattered," but Krassner told me it meant "dirty." I think it fits both ways.

'Day of Judgment Upon Us,' " — Gary Snyder read by Elmer
Gantry. Now we're all into it. The Old Left is very up tight.
They say we are sent by the CIA.

The kids laugh. "Why don't you guys give away acid the
way you do food?"

"Well, we gave out 5,000 capsules at the Be-In last month."

The Old Left is shitting, really scared of acid. They are losing control, Marx with flowers in his hair, can't deal with con-
tradictory stimuli, simultaneous bombardment. Marxism is
irrelevant to the U.S.A., as irrelevant as Capitalism.

The Diggers left after we had talked the whole night. The
SDS'ers slept all night very soundly. They had nothing to talk
about in those wee morning hours when you rap on and on and
a dialogue of non-verbal vibrations begins. You Relate!! You
Plan!! You Think!! You get Stoned!! You Feel!! And SDS sleeps
in beds with clean sheets they have brought because they know
how to "do" conferences. The Old Left snoozes in the best beds
in the house. They have to get their sleep so they can run back
to their nice fat system jobs, "burrowing from within," asking
the Negroes (now called Blacks) to do it for them, the Negroes, the students, the workers, anybody but them. They want
to discuss "Yankee Imperialism." All the old Jewish Leftists are
a little nervous about the Middle East business. It was obvious
by the way it was avoided. Lost a lot of Jewish pacifists in the
last few weeks.

The seminars drag on ... a total bore ... Jim and I are
avoided, except by a small group. They do socialism, we blow
pot in the grass, they do imperialism, we go swimming, they
do racism, we do flowers for everybody and clean up the rooms.

Back to the Conference: Hayden asked, "How do you make it
stick, how do you prevent cooptation? I thought he said *copu-
lation*. I answered that you build a better system. Assume
America is already dead, dead for those kids who are flocking
to the Lower East Side and Haight-Ashbury, and give them a

new, positive, authentic frame of reference. If it's done effec-
tively they won't go back. What is there to go back to? And
the kids are flocking in or dropping out by the droves, on their
way to San Francisco, on their way to New York. The media
does it for us. Wow! "If you're going to San Francisco, be sure
to wear a flower in your hair." That's Number 1 in the country.
The media is the message. Use it! No fundraising, no full-page
ads in the N.Y. *Times,* no press releases. Just do your thing;
the press eats it up. MAKE NEWS.

   Quote: "Pot feels good, it's fun to turn on."
They print it, not aware of the disruption they cause. The press
spreads the word, tells them where the action is and they leave
America. They stream to its two shores, can't go any further,
up against the ocean, what to do, down and out. "There's a
new world somewhere, if you will only hold my hand," sings
the radio just as I write this line. Man, it's all around us. Total
bombardment . . . can it lead to total commitment? New forms
emerge. S.F. and N.Y. become the schools. The streets are the
classrooms, religion's in your head.

   We sit on the tribal council, Indian circle, incense burning,
soft lights. The first person speaks for as long as he wants, then
the next, no interruptions, consensus is reached, respect for
other heads is achieved, we can do, we can be community.
There are no problems, only things to do. Tribes give inner
guidance, activists give helping hands to newcomers. We grow,
we multiply, we build on the ashes of the old. The structure of
the meeting (read Paul Goodman, *Utopian Ideas and Prac-
tical Proposals*) gives a clue to where its collective head is at.
Ours is a circle: respect, love, trust, delicate. A black meeting
image: sweat, yelling, stomping, "Burn, baby, burn."

   Two nights ago spoke at the *Catholic Worker.* Loved it, con-
verts to be won, dialogue to be opened. Structure sloppy, irreg-
ular tables, people on floor, on tables, image — dedication,
doing, primitive. Dorothy Day is a Digger. Last night at Hudson Institute think tank. Herman Kahn's brain session: long

tables arranged in a square panel. We sit apart in the back of
the room — niggers to the end. Angry at myself for going. Col-
laborating with the enemy for ego purposes. They want to
know how strong we are, we put them on; we are ridiculous,
ignore us, Herman Kahn. Look how freaky we are with our
flowers and bells. We know we're right. One of the members
confesses to me, "We're glad you brought your girl friends.
They are a lot prettier than ours." Of course they are, they are
beautiful women, we are beautiful men. You guys are fags,
machines. We end up at a drive-in movie digging Elvis Presley.

June 24, 1967

Writing on the run or rather fly as I speed back from San
Francisco across America. John Wayne in *El Dorado* just
ended and my mind is filled with guns — long guns, shotguns,
derringers, machine guns. "You bettah get yourself a gun,
boy . . ." Rap Brown, John Wayne, Diggers. Even Marvin Garson got himself a rifle, and he points it out in the bay at huge
aircraft carriers filled with death bound for the war out
there. "Is there really a war out there?" I sit in this airplane
on imitation leather seats, looking up plastic stewardesses'
skirts, at executive playing out his fantasy in the *Wall Street
Journal*, at triple chins of tight-assed old hag who gobbles her
dietary ulcer lunch. You bet your ass this country is involved
in an evil war. I'd never have to leave this seat to know that,
never have to read a newspaper.

We are throwing everything we've got at the Pentagon — evil
hulk that sits like a cancerous death-trap on the beautiful Po-

tomac. An Exorcism to cast out the evil spirits on October 21st. The Pentagon shall not survive, neither for that matter will the fag-ridden peace movement. "Ring-around-the-Pentagon-a-pocket-full-of-pot." Wrote a beautiful poem that I lost last week when Marty Carey and I got arrested there. Met a Digger in San Francisco who went to the Chicago New Politics mess. He sat on the stage with a flute in one hand and a tire iron in the other, drawing an imaginary circle around himself. "I declare this area a liberated zone. Anyone enters and I'll kill him." A total political stance. I am ready for the struggle. As far as the revolution goes, it started when I was born. Broke with the Mobilization coalition for Washington (which means I don't go to their meetings anymore). At one meeting I declared, "The truth lies through insanity." They are scared shitless of the mystery. They suppressed an article by Keith Lampe because of the word "SUCK." My Lord, what fucking prudes. Our suck magic is much too strong medicine for the middle-class peace movement.

Many wild happenings are planned in preparation: circling of Washington Monument, Empire State Building (vertically), Make Love Day orgy leading up to October 21st. On Columbus Day a mighty caravan of wagons will roll East out of San Francisco to rediscover America complete with real live Indian scouts, compliments of Chief Rolling Thunder of the Shoshone. Junk cars, stolen buses, motorcycles, rock bands, flower banners, dope, incense, and enough food for the long journey. Wagon train East. Yahoo! We will dye the Potomac red, burn the cherry trees, panhandle embassies, attack with water pistols, marbles, bubble gum wrappers, bazookas, girls will run naked and piss on the Pentagon walls, sorcerers, swamis, witches, voodoo, warlocks, medicine men, and speed freaks will hurl their magic at the faded brown walls. Rock bands will bomb out with "Joshua fit the Battle of Jericho." We will dance and sing and chant the mighty OM. We will fuck on the grass and beat ourselves against the doors. Everyone will scream "VOTE FOR ME." We shall raise the flag of nothingness over the

Pentagon and a mighty cheer of liberation will echo through the land. "We are Free, Great God Almighty, Free at last." Schoolchildren will rip out their desks and throw ink at stunned instructors, office secretaries will disrobe and run into the streets, newsboys will rip up their newspapers and sit on the curbstones masturbating, storekeepers will throw open their doors making everything free, accountants will all collapse in one mighty heart attack, soldiers will throw down their guns. "The War is over. Let's get some ass." No permits, no N.Y. *Times* ads, no mailing lists, no meetings. It will happen because the time is ripe. Come to the Day of Judgment. Forget about degrees, they are useless scraps of paper. Turn them into Litter Art. Don't hold back. Let the baby-Beatles shut your mouth and open your mind. On October 6th the Diggers in S.F. will present the Death of the Hippie and the Birth of the Free Man. S.F. will become the first Free City extending the boundaries of the Haight-Ashbury ghetto. Extend all boundaries, blow your mind. Conversation between me and other:

> OTHER: What do you want?
>
> ME: To win.
>
> OTHER: To win what?
>
> ME: Fuck you!

Skulldiggery shoots up the media. Chaos. Riots, earthquakes, black men grabbed in Philadelphia with enough poison for 4,000 people or cops, Digger hurls pie at colonel at University of California. "Splash." Last night at the Straight Theater in Haight-Ashbury sheer beauty of mind-body dancers acting out fears of paranoid America, huddled in a corner and casual as can be they take their clothes off and continue the dance. "We are free, we are Men, we are Women, we love, we hate, we are real" — plastic-coated America. America let's see your balls, America can I only see them on a tiny screen in a superjet acted out by John Wayne and Robert Mitchum in a land called El Dorado. El Dorado is now at the Straight Theater and it's all free.

September 28, 1967

A GOOD AD FOR THE EXORCISM

Don't miss *Bonnie and Clyde*
Don't miss STP
Don't miss getting laid
Don't miss lion steak
Don't miss Allen Ginsberg
Don't miss Billy the Kid
Don't miss Ché Guevara
Don't miss the Exorcism of the
                                    in living color

                    October 21, 1967

HOW I LOST THE WAR
AT THE PENTAGON

Artaud is alive at the walls of the Pentagon, bursting the seams of conventional protest, injecting new blood into the peace movement. Real blood, symbolic blood and — for camouflage —Dayglo blood. Something for everybody.

Homecoming Day at the Pentagon and the cheerleaders chant "Beat Army! Beat Army!" It's SDS at the 30-yard line and third down. Robin cuts the rope with a hunting knife and the Charge of the Flower Brigade is on.

One longhair smashes a window and is beaten to the ground. The Pentagon vibrates and begins to rise in the air. Someone gives a marshal a leaflet on U.S. imperialism, another squirts him with LACE, a high potency sex juice that makes you "pull your clothes off and make love" (according to *Time* magazine), people are stuffing flowers in rifle barrels, protesters throw tear gas at each other (according to the Washington *Post*).

A girl unzips an MP's fly and Sergeant Pepper asks the band to play *The Star Spangled Banner.* They lay down their Viet Cong flags and pick up their instruments. *Oh, say, can you see* . . . When it's over someone yells, "Play ball!" — and the pushing and shoving begins again.

FLASHBACK: Baby and I, complete with Uncle Sam hats and Flower Flags, jump a barbed-wire fence and are quickly surrounded by marshals and soldiers.

"We're Mr. and Mrs. America, and we claim this land in the name of Free America."

We plant the Flag and hold our ground. The troops are really shook. Do you club Uncle Sam? We're screaming incantations.

"You're under arrest. What's your name?"

Mr. and Mrs. America, and Mrs. America's pregnant."

The troops lower their clubs in respect. A marshal writes in his book: "Mr. and Mrs. America — Trespassing." We sit down and make love. Another marshal unarrests us. A lieutenant arrests us. A corporal unarrests us. We continue making love.

After about 20 minutes we stand and offer to shake hands with the marshals. They refuse. We walk away glowing, off to liberate another zone. The crowd cheers. "You can do anything you want, baby, it's a free country. Just do it, don't bullshit."

The peace movement has gone crazy and it's about time. Our alternative fantasy will match in zaniness the war in Vietnam. Fantasy is Freedom. Anybody can do anything. "The Pentagon will rise 300 feet in the air."

No rules, speeches won't do, leaders are all full of shit. Pull your clothes off (*Make Love, Not War*), punch a marshal, jump a wall, do a dance, sing a song, paint the building, blow it up, charge and get inside.

FLASHBACK: "67-68-69-70-"

"What do you think you guys are doing?"

"Measuring the Pentagon. We have to see how many people we'll need to form a ring around it."

"You're what!"

"It's very simple. You see, the Pentagon is a symbol of evil in most religions. You're religious, aren't you?"

"Unh."

"Well, the only way to exorcise the evil spirits here is to form a circle around the Pentagon. 87-88-89 . . ."

The two scouts are soon surrounded by a corps of guards, FBI agents, soldiers and some mighty impressive brass.

"*112-113-114-*"

"Are you guys serious? It's against the law to measure the Pentagon."

"Are you guys serious? Show us the law. *237-238-239-240.* That does it. Colonel, how much is *240* times *5?*"

"What? What the hell's going on here!"

"1200," answers Bruce, an impressive-looking agent who tells us later he works in a security department that doesn't even have a name yet.

We show them our exorcism flyers. They bust us for littering.

"Shades of Alice's Restaurant. Are you guys kidding? That ain't litter, it's art."

"Litter."

"Art."

"Litter."

"How about Litter Art?" says Bruce after two hours.

We are free to go, but have to be very sneaky and ditch Bruce somewhere inside the Pentagon maze so he won't find the Acapulco Gold in the car.

The magic is beginning to work, but the media must be convinced. You simply cannot call them up and say, "Pardon me, but the Pentagon will rise in the air on October 21st." You've got to show them.

Friday, the 13th, Village Theater, warlocks, witches, speed freaks, Fugs and assorted kooks plus one non-believer named Krassner. "Out, Demons, Out!" — and, *zip*, up goes the mock Pentagon. "Higher! Higher! Higher!"

(Is it legal to cry *Higher* in a crowded theater?)

We burn the model and will use its ashes on Big Daddy the following week. Media is free. Use it. Don't pay for it. Don't buy ads. Make news.

FLASHBACK: "Give me the City Desk . . . Hello. I've defected from the Diggers because they have this new sex drug called LACE. They plan to use it at the Pentagon. It's against my morals to use it on people against their will, so I want to confess. It's got LSD and DMSO, a penetrating agent. It's lysergic acid crypto ethelene and it's purple. Why don't you come over and I'll show you how it works."

The press conference is at 8 P.M. Two couples sit on a

couch. The four are squirted with the purple liquid. It disappears into their skin. They look dazed. Like robots they slowly peel off their clothes. The reporters pant. Like non-robots they begin to fuck. After a half hour the drug has worn off.

"Any questions, gentlemen?"

LACE, the new love drug, goes to the Pentagon.

This exorcism business is getting pretty exciting. Let's see *Progressive Labor* match LACE. The Pentagon happening transcended the issue of the War. *The War Is Over*, sings Phil Ochs, and the protest becomes directed to the entire fabric of a restrictive, dull, brutal society.

The protesters become total political animals.

A totality emerges that renders the word *political* meaningless. "The war is over." Everybody's yelling and screaming. Someone writes *LBJ loves Ho Chi Minh* on the wall.

Ring around the Pentagon, a pocket full of pot
Four and twenty generals all begin to rot.
All the evil spirits start to tumble out
Now the war is over, we all begin to shout.

The soldiers have a choice. "Join us! Join us!" — the cry goes up. Three do. Drop their helmets and guns and break ranks. They are caught by the marshals and dragged away into oblivion and the third degree.

It's the sixth hour of my trip. A super one, helped by large doses of revolution, no food or water, and a small purple tablet popped in my mouth by Charlie from the San Francisco *Oracle*.

A sense of integration possesses me that comes from pissing on the Pentagon: combining biological necessity with emotional feeling.

Baby and I retreat to the bowels of D.C. and grab a night's sleep after an orgy of champagne poured from an MP's helmet. It sure is one hell of a revolution.

Worried parents call the Defense Department to see if their children have been arrested and are given the number of the National Mobilization's office.

We come prepared to give our lives and debate the morality of parking on a crosswalk.

FLASHBACK: Sunday at the Pentagon is a different scene. A mind trip working on the troops. Ex-soldiers talk to MPs. So do girls, college kids and priests, for twelve long hours. Talking, singing, sharing, contrasting Free America vs. the Uniformed Machine. At midnight the Pentagon speaks after two days of silence.

"Your permit has expired. If you do not leave the area you will be arrested. All demonstrators are requested to leave the area at once. This is a recorded announcement."

"Fuck you, Pentagon. I'm not a demonstrator. I'm a tourist."

Everybody is herded into vans. The door slams shut but the lock doesn't work.

"The New Action Army sure is a pisser."

The MPs laugh and finally get the bolt in place. Off we go to Occoquan and jail land. "Carry me back to Ol' Virginny . . ." I hate jail. I try to chew my way through the van door and am doing pretty well when some of the girls get scared.

I get processed through as FREE Digger. "I'm a girl," I insist when one of the marshals gives me the clue. A matron peeks and discovers differently. "No, honey, I'm just flatchested, honest."

Jail is a goof. Easiest jailing of all time. The Army is into brainwashing. Clean sheets, good breakfast, propaganda radio station.

We call the guard and demand to be treated as prisoners of war. He listens patiently as we ask for the International Red Cross and other courtesies accorded under the Geneva Convention. He scratches his head and walks away.

Three guys begin to dig a tunnel. Everybody's trying to remember Stalag 17. At four o'clock I'm led out, meet my baby and we go to court. "The family that disobeys together stays together." Even the judge laughs, says ten bucks each and we're free.

Everybody's making the sign of the V. The battle is over. The question everyone's asking is when's the next happening?

Small battles will occur in countless communities around the country; most centered at local induction centers.

Two days after the Pentagon three clergymen walk into the induction center in Baltimore and dump blood in the files. Blood! "You bet your ass — that's what war's about, isn't it?"

New York treated Dean Rusk to a bloodbath on November 14th at the Hilton Hotel. Organized by the newly formed Protesters, Troublemakers and Anarchists. Headlines blare: "Cops Bust Up PTA Meeting."

Jesus visits St. Patrick's Cathedral. How about running Shirley Temple for Congress again? Pickets at Bellevue shout "Free LBJ!" A scenario at campus recruiting tables might include a tent with soft music and girls in bikinis. That's a real alternative.

Oh, by the way, January is Alien Registration Month. See you at the Post Office.

Get ready for a big event at the Democratic National Convention in Chicago next August. How about a truly open convention? Thousands of *Vote for Me* buttons, everybody prints his own campaign literature and distributes pictures of themselves. Then we all rush the convention, get to the rostrum and nominate ourselves.

After all, it seems the only cat who lives for nothing in this country is LBJ. I've never met anyone who has ever seen him pay for anything. He doesn't even have a wallet. So if you want to live free, then stand up proudly on that convention platform, but don't start your speech with "My friends, come, let us reason together," or you'll lose the election.

November 18, 1967

I'm sitting here in Room 219, 100 Centre Street, waiting to go
to trial. I've been here so often, the Security guards call me by
my first name. It's the usual northern courtroom scene: Ninety-
year-old judge hunched over the bench; lawyers scuttling around
the pit with paper and briefcases, all got brown suits (whatever happened to gray flannels?); the pews are filled with the
usual number of Puerto Ricans, black people, and a scattering
of longhairs. The wall behind the judge says, in gold letters
(so help me dog) IN GOD WE RUST.

Yesterday down the hall Allen Ginsberg read a blistering
poem, to the disgust of the cops and the cheers of the peace
demonstrators, pickpockets, prostitutes, dope pushers, and card
hustlers. In Newark I hear they go one better and the judge
reads the defendant's poetry to him. (Leroi Jones's trial.) After
waiting six hours for a hearing I get a postponement because
the judge came two hours late to court. I'm in no hurry. The
charge is hitting a cop with a bottle. . . .

It is a chilly night. Dean Rusk has come to town. We ren-
dezvous at 57th Street and Seventh Avenue, blocks away from
the Hilton. Some of us recognize each other. Demonstrations
always have a reunion atmosphere. Most people got army jack-
ets; there are more longhairs than I expected. Everybody's got
a prop: plastic bags filled with blood, smoke bombs, flares.
Scouts run down the blocks scouting the enemy's position, and
report back. There are about a hundred of us now, and the
scouts also report bands of rovers at three or four other inter-
sections. We decide to hit the intersection at 6 P.M. sharp.

Someone suggests attacking only limousines and Cadillacs. Suddenly the intersection erupts. Cars jam up. Horns beep. Smoke bombs go off. Flares are lit. A straight couple ask me what's going on? I shout, "There's a WAR on! Can't you see?" A long black limousine has blood splattered on its window and *Peace* in Day-glo letters sprayed on its trunk lid. "Let's get out of here," someone yells and everyone runs toward Sixth Avenue. It's a wild scene. Cops charging people, demonstrators, Christmas shoppers, people going to hear Dean Rusk. Cops in formation wading into crowds, clubbing away. The crowd retreats to the sidewalk and cops on horses move right in on them. Crunch! Kids lying in the street bleeding all over. One's out colder than a mackerel. We rush out to pull him in when out of nowhere this guy grabs me from behind.

I think he is a right-wing heckler, and we're having a fist fight when the blue boys arrive. It seems he is a plain-clothesman. Before I know it I'm standing in the 16th Precinct, and Badge #26466, who has missed some of the action, kicks me in the nuts. In the back room three cops are working over one demonstrator who has his arms handcuffed behind his back. They beat him for a good ten minutes with fists and clubs. All the cops are aching for blood. One is yelling how his brother got killed in Vietnam and challenges anybody to a fight in the back alley. They call us "scum-bags" and "fairies" and "Jew-bastards" and "commies" and one says, "You pull dese guys' pants off and they ain't got no pecker, just a little piece of flesh." There are other swears that I couldn't even recognize because of the culture gap but it seems they sure got this sex hang-up. Pretty soon we're all herded into a van. All except the guy who got beat up real bad. They want to clean him up a bit before sending him down. In the Tombs we are put in a special block with other demonstrators. It's old home week and everybody's cheering and making the V sign and singing old freedom songs and Beatle tunes. I'm sitting next to a seventeen-year-old kid.

"What they grab you for?"

"Breaking a window. I just jumped up on this Cadillac and kicked in the window."

"That's pretty far out. You go to the Pentagon?"

"No, this is my first demonstration."

I kind of nodded and leaned my aching head back against the wall. Ron Carver, from Columbia SDS, was leading an old one, "We'll never turn back." It sort of separates the veterans from the newcomers, it being the theme song of the Mississippi Project and all that. It sure made a body reminisce. I knew Ron in SNCC and then up in a peace campaign in Massachusetts in '66. He's like about a hundred other veterans I know who are still active. We rarely see each other except at demonstrations. This isn't some vast organized conspiracy, like most people think, just a lot of guys whose heads are in the same place but with different styles. Ron and I talk with our eyes. We're brothers. We've been through this so many times it's routine. We're both working out the strategy for our next street scene even as we finish the sad "We'll never turn back" and swing into "This little light of mine."

"You hair's gettin' longer," he jokes.

"Yeah, I'm a flower child."

December 10, 1967

3

THE NEW NIGGERS

February 16, 1968

Stokely:

It's been a year since I last saw you in Washington and a lot has happened. I have left Liberty House to others. It is going well, but PPC has just been able to hold its own in Mississippi. Living on the Lower East Side I was naturally aware of this whole hippie business and started to organize around here: bail funds, Free Stores, smoke-ins, be-ins. We threw out money at the stock exchange in a wild event I'm sure you heard about. We threw soot on Con Ed executives and dumped smoke bombs in their lobby. Exorcising the Pentagon of its evil spirits, back to New York and a blood bath for Dean Rusk in which we threw seventeen gallons of blood at cops, Rusk, limousines. Lots of other things. I'm enclosing an article for you to read and maybe comment on.

We are working on a huge Youth Festival in Chicago at the time of the Democratic Convention. I hope I get to participate. I'm currently on trial for supposedly hitting a cop with a bottle in a demonstration. I can't imagine what they are talking about, me being a flower child and all that. I am also working on getting a group of longhairs along with a rock band to visit Cuba. I hear Castro is interested. I have been reading a good deal about Cuba and having talks with its UN Embassy. I would very much like to go. Julius Lester and I talked the other night about it. I see Mendy Sampstein every once in awhile but he has a job as a cab driver and isn't involved in the Movement any more. I saw you in a movie by Peter Brook last night. It was a rotten movie — very boring. Nothing like *Planet of the Apes*, which is a trip and a half. I was in Washington last week, we busted up McCarthy's talk with some guerrilla theater. I tried to call you but you are hard to find. I thought your book was blah compared to some exciting TV shots of your talk in France with a huge photo of Ché behind you. I heard you and Emmett Grogan didn't get along too well in England? That's too bad if it's true 'cause Grogan is OK. I see Timothy Leary a lot. He has

has just done a whole turnabout. He's supporting Gregory for President and joining us in bringing people to Chicago. His little drop-out shelter in Millbrook gets busted about once a week by the cops and it's had an effect in getting him involved. I would like very much to talk to you if you come to New York. Maybe a get-together down here. I got some fantastic stuff that a friend brought back from Vietnam and it ain't napalm. It'll make your ears fall off.

In freedom,

GARBAGE

Linn House, ex-editor of *Innerspace*, once said that you could tell a good deal about people by what they did with their garbage. On a chilly night last December a demonstration was going on at the Ninth Precinct. In one week four Digger-sponsored crash pads were busted by the cops. Without search warrants, the police kicked in the doors and grabbed anyone who looked under eighteen. No search warrants were needed because these were not really arrests, since runaways are returned to their parents or sent to a youth house. This night four people were being held captive and everyone agreed to walk into the police station confessing that they too were runaways and demand that the police call their parents. The police would have no part of this, though, and after arresting a few souls threw everyone out of the station. People started to shout and sing and someone wrote COPS SUCK on a police car and when the police started to push everyone away people ran up Second Avenue throwing trash cans into the street. In ten minutes Second Avenue was covered under a sea of garbage.

The intriguing element of this act was that these were the same merry souls who just eight months ago were participating in a huge Sweep-In just two blocks south of the same Precinct. In both cases the garbage was used as a theatrical prop in making a statement. In the Sweep-In we were saying: If you include an element of joy, people will be willing to show some interest in their community, and they will perform tasks the society considers menial, for free. It also says something about a city government that can let over thirty tons of garbage go unnoticed on a street six blocks long. When the garbage was thrown in the street the message was the opposite: you mess with us and we'll mess with you. Both acts were acts of love. Both acts are saying we have a community.

Similar circumstances exist at public events. For example, it makes perfectly good sense to pick up the trash at the Monterey Pops Festival and leave it on the ground at the Pentagon demonstration. There is creative construction but there is also creative destruction. A community not prepared to pick up its garbage cannot survive and neither can a community not prepared to defend itself.°

TALKING IN MY SLEEP — AN EXERCISE IN SELF-CRITICISM

A mythical interview of questions that are asked and answers that are given. Interviews are always going on. Here's one with myself.

° As I write this, 100,000 tons of garbage are piled up on the streets of New York. I have a vision of the country being totally inundated under this massive garbage pile. Future historians would write that America was destroyed by a nuclear attack when in actuality the people just stopped picking up their trash.

Do you have an ideology?
No. Ideology is a brain disease.

Do you have a movement?
Yes. It's called Dancing.

Isn't that a put-on?
No.

Can you explain that?
Suppose we start the questions again.

OK. Do you have an ideology?
We are for peace, equal rights, and brotherhood.

Now I understand.
I don't. That was a put-on. I don't understand what I said.

I'm getting confused.
Well, let's go on.

Are you for anything? Do you have a vision of this new society you talk of?
Yes. We are for a free society.

Could you spell that out?
F-R-E-E.

What do you mean free?
You know what that means. America: the land of the free. Free means you don't pay, doesn't it?

Yes, I guess so. Do you mean all the goods and services would be free?
Precisely. That's what the technological revolution would produce if we let it run unchecked. If we stopped trying to control it.

What controls it?
The profit incentive, I guess. Property hang-ups. One task we have is to separate the concept of productivity from work. Work is money. Work is postponement of pleasure. Work is always done for someone else: the boss, the kids, the guy next door. Work is competition. Work was linked to productivity to serve the Industrial Revolution. We must separate the two. We must abolish work and all the drudgery it represents.

Who will do what we now call dirty work, like picking up the garbage?
Well, there are a lot of possibilities. There won't be any dirty work. If you're involved in a revolution you have a different attitude toward work. It is not separate from your vision . . . All work now is dirty work. Lots of people might dig dealing with garbage. Maybe there won't be any garbage. Maybe we'll just let it pile up. Maybe everybody will have a garbage disposal. There are numerous possibilities.

Don't you think competition leads to productivity?
Well, I think it did during the Industrial Revolution but it won't do for the future. Competition also leads to war. Cooperation will be the motivating factor in a free society. I think cooperation is more akin to the human spirit. Competition is grafted on by institutions, by a capitalist economy, by religion, by schools. Every institution I can think of in this country promotes competition.

Are you a communist?
Are you an anti-communist?

Does it matter?
Well, I'm tempted to say Yes if I sense you are. I remember when I was young I would only say I was Jewish if I thought the person asking the question was anti-Semitic.

What do you think of Russia?
Ugh! Same as here. Dull, bureaucratic-sterile-puritanical. Do
you remember when Kosygin came here and met with Johnson
in New Jersey? They looked the same. They think the same.
Neither way the wave of the future. Johnson is a communist.

What is the wave of the future?
The National Liberation Front, the Cuban Revolution, the
young here and around the world.

Doesn't everybody always place great hope in the young?
Yes, I think so. But young people today are very different from
previous generations. I think generational revolt has gone on
throughout history. Ortega y Gasset in *Man and Crisis* shows that
very dramatically. But there are significant differences. The
hydrogen bomb, TV, satellites, jet planes — everything is more
immediate, more involving. We are the first internationalists.
Vietnam rice paddies are as real to me as the Empire State
Building. If you don't live in New York, maybe they are more
real. We live in a global village.

Do you like McLuhan?
Let's say I think he is more relevant than Marx. Quentin Fiore,
his assistant, is more McLuhan than McLuhan. He's the one
who puts the ideas into action. McLuhan still struggles with the
printed word. But he is an explorer. He experiments. For an old
guy he does well. He understands how to communicate information. It's just that his living style — Catholic, university life,
grants, the risks that he takes — is merely academic. Let's say I
respect him, but don't love him. What we seek are new living
styles. We don't want to talk about them. We want to live them.

Do you consider what you are doing politically relevent?
No.

Is that the best answer you can think of?
Well, when you ask a question like that you trigger off umpteen responses in my head. I believe in the politics of ecstasy.

Can you explain that a little more?
No, but I can touch it, I can smell it, I can even dance it. I can even fight it. Politics to me is the way somebody lives his life. Not what they vote for or support or even believe in. I'm more interested in art than politics but, well, see, we are all caught in a word box. I find it difficult to make these kinds of divisions. Northrop, in *Meeting of East and West*, said, "Life is an undifferentiated aesthetic continuum." Let me say that the Vietcong attacking the U.S. Embassy in Saigon is a work of art. I guess I like revolutionary art.

This word game, as you call it. Doesn't that present problems in conveying what you want to say?
Yes, but not in what I want to do. Let me say . . . Did you ever hear Andy Warhol talk?

Yes, or at least I think it was him.
Well, I would like to combine his style and that of Castro's. Warhol understands modern media. Castro has the passion for social change. It's not easy. One's a fag and the other is the epitome of virility. If I was forced to make the choice I would choose Castro, but right now in this period of change in the country the styles of the two can be blended. It's not guerrilla warfare but, well, maybe a good term is monkey warfare. If the country becomes more repressive we must become Castros. If it becomes more tolerant we must become Warhols.

Do you see the country becoming more repressive?
Well, it's very hard to be objective about that. The cops around here are certainly a bunch of bastards. It's winter now and traditionally that's a time of paranoia because it's a time of less action than the summer. Everything has always been geared to the

summer. School's out. People in the streets. More action. When
you are involved you don't get paranoid. It's when you sit back
and try to figure out what's going on, or what you should do.
The winter is the hardest time for revolutionists in this country.
We probably should hibernate. Everything builds toward the
summer. This year it seems more so. Everyday we talk of Chicago and the Festival. Everyday the news carries a prediction
of the "long hot summer." The other day I saw a report from
Detroit. People, one white line, one black line, lining up at a
gun shop. Meanwhile the mayor is trying to cool things with a
nice friendly speech on brotherhood. It was some contrast.
Every day has a new report on some new police weapon system.
Then there is uncertainty and the tendency to re-examine your
tactics. Right now I feel like Dwight Eisenhower on an acid
trip. "On the one hand this — on the other hand that." I think
it's a case of information overload. See, I am conditioned to perform well in chaos — actual chaos. Say a riot. In a riot I know
exactly what to do. I'm not good for the winter. This is my last
winter in the North. I have to live in total summer if I am to
survive.

Will the summer action bring on more repression?
Oh, I suppose so. I see this country as getting simultaneously
more repressive and more tolerant. People run off to Hanoi to
collaborate with the enemy. Everybody's smoking pot on the
streets. People go on TV and radio shows and spell out in detail
plans of sabotage. And simultaneously there is repression. The
combination of the two is going to produce highly volatile conditions and that's why many different tactics are needed. Right
now revolution is anything you can get away with. It has to be
that way because of the nature of the opposition.

What is going to accelerate that process?
Well, Vietnam, the black revolution, and most importantly, WE
ARE! All three present this system with more unsolvable prob-
lems than it can deal with. You see, there is no solution to the

Vietnam war. To leave or to stay is a defeat. No matter what the government does in the ghettos it loses. More aid programs increase the appetite for more demands. More repression produces more anger and defensive violence. The same with the young. I know a girl, Peggy Dobbins, who was a teacher at Brooklyn College. She let the students determine the curriculum; before you knew it, the students wanted to grade themselves. She agreed to go along and of course got the ax from the administration. The more you get, the more you want. The more you are prevented from getting what you want, the more you fight to get it. These are trends that are irreversible, because the government cannot deal with these problems — I mean, the government "deals" with problems rather than solving them.

That's pretty political in its analysis. It's New Left in its wording.
Ah, well, it's a regression. I haven't presented any new ideas. But, well, that's the point. All the ideas are in and have been for some time. I guess I just rap on that from force of habit. I was once in the New Left but I outgrew it. Or perhaps it outgrew me. We differ on many things.

Like what?
Fun. I think fun and leisure are great. I don't like the concept of a movement built on sacrifice, dedication, responsibility, anger, frustration and guilt. All those down things. I would say, Look, you want to have more fun, you want to get laid more, you want to turn on with friends, you want an outlet for your creativity, then get out of school, quit your job. Come on out and help build and defend the society you want. Stop trying to organize everybody but yourself. Begin to live your vision. For example, the other night I was at a benefit for a peace group. Great music, light shows, friends all over the place. It was a good time. Some of the money raised goes to arrange rallies at which speakers give boring political speeches. People think it's a drag but that's the sacrifice to get out the politically

relevant statement. The point is, nobody listens to politically relevant statements. In Chicago we'll have a huge free music festival. Everyone already knows our feelings on the issues because we are there. It will have a tremendous impact if we can also project the image that we are having all the fun too. When I say fun, I mean an experience so intense that you actualize your full potential. You become LIFE. LIFE IS FUN. Political irrelevance is more effective than political relevance.

I notice as we get further into the interview that your answers get more linear and longer.
You're observant. I'm getting tired.

A few more: I hear you're writing a book. What's it about?
Well, it's called *Revolution for the Hell of It*. Sometimes I think I'm writing it just to see that title on a book jacket. Actually, if I have my way, the book jacket won't have the title on it. The book jacket will have two sleeves, a collar, buttons down the front, and the word BOOK on the back.

Why are you writing it?
Well, 'cause I have no idea how to make a movie. It has some parts I like but the book form is difficult and I write on the run. There is also the time gap. You know, months of delay before it comes out. By then it's a whole new ball game. As far as the medium of print is concerned, I would say I like free street leaflets the best.

Which medium do you like the best of all?
Making love.

Anything else?
Well, I like to experience pleasure, to have fun. I enjoy blowing people's minds. You know, walking up to somebody and saying, "Would you hold this dollar for me while I go in that store and steal something?" The crazier the better. I like being crazy.

Letting go. Losing control. Just doing what pops into my mind.
I trust my impulses. I find the less I try to think through a situation, the better it comes off.

**I've seen things you've written under other names. Is that part
of the put-on?**
I do that a lot. It is fun because I really get pleasure in doing
the act or helping to see it come off. Using false names or other
people's makes sense to me. I'm not so sure about it now. You
get known. As soon as you do anything in this country you become a celebrity. It's not really the same as being a leader. You
can only stimulate actions. Stopping them or controlling them
is something leaders can do. I'm not a leader. Nobody is under
my command. I haven't the vaguest idea how to stop a demonstration, say, except to go home. I'm really not interested in
stopping anything, so I'm not a leader. But this celebrity thing
has certain problems. Using false names just tends to increase
the myth after a while. Sometimes I do now, and sometimes I
don't. If I can get away with it, I do.

Will you use a false name on the book?
If I can get away with it.

**Isn't this celebrity or star system alien to your visions of a new
society?**
Most definitely. I find as you get more and more well known
you get less personal freedom. You spend more time doing other
people's things than your own. You know, people calling in the
middle of the night with their problems. Imagine this scene:
You are trying to steal some groceries and some old lady comes
up and says how much she likes what you're doing. That's why
I use disguises, so I can keep in shape by having to hustle without the myth. The day I can't shoplift, panhandle, or pass out
leaflets on my own is the day I'll retire. The myth, like everything else, is free. Anybody can claim he is it and use it to
hustle.

What's the solution? Is there any to the celebrity game?
I don't know. I envision a new life after Chicago. I don't intend
to deal with symbolic confrontations. I'm interested in just living with a few friends and building a community. If there is to
be confrontation, let it be with the local sheriff rather than LBJ.
Maybe this is just a fantasy, though. Maybe it won't happen. I
guess everyone dreams of a peaceful life in the country. Especially in the winter.

You're planning to drop out?
Well, dropping out is a continual process. I don't see anything
really definite in the future. I just don't want to get boxed-in to
playing a predetermined role. Let's say, so much of what we do
is theater — in life I just don't want to get caught in a Broadway
show that lasts five years, even if it is a success. The celebrity
bag is another form of careerism. But you see, celebrity status is
very helpful in working with media. It's my problem and I'll
deal with it just like any other problem. I'll do the best I can.

**Is that why the Yippies were created? To manipulate the
media?**
Exactly. You see, we are faced with this task of getting huge
numbers of people to come to Chicago along with hundreds of
performers, artists, theater groups, engineers. Essentially, people involved in trying to work out a new society. How do you
do this starting from scratch, with no organization, no money,
nothing? Well, the answer is that you create a myth. Something
that people can play a role in, can relate to. This is especially
true of media people. I'll give you an example. A reporter was
interviewing us once and he liked what we were doing. He said
"I'm going to tell what good ideas you guys really have. I'm going to tell the truth about the Yippies." We said, "That won't
help a bit. Lie about us." It doesn't matter as long as he gets
Yippie! and Chicago linked together in a magical way. The
myth is about LIFE vs. DEATH. That's why we are headed for
a powerful clash.

You don't want the truth told?

Well, I don't want to get philosophical but there is really no such animal. Especially when one talks of creating a myth. How can you have a true myth? When newspapers distort a story they become participants in the creation of the myth. We love distortions. Those papers that claim to be accurate, *i.e.*, the New York *Times, Village Voice, Ramparts, The Nation, Commentary,* that whole academic word scene is a total bore. In the end they probably distort things more than the *Daily News*. The New York *Times* is the American Establishment, not the *Daily News.* The *Daily News* creates a living style. You know: "Pot-smoking, dirty, beatnik, pinko, sex-crazy, Vietnik, so-called Yippies." Compare that to the New York *Times*: "Members of the newly formed Youth International Party (YIP)." The New York *Times* is death. The *Daily News* is the closest thing to TV. Look at its front page, always a big picture. It looks like a TV set. I could go on and on about this. It's a very important point. Distortion is essential to myth-making.

Are you saying that you actually like the *Daily News?*

Not exactly, but I don't consider it the enemy, in the same way that I don't consider George Wallace the enemy. Corporate liberalism, Robert Kennedy, Xerox, David Susskind, the New York *Times*, Harvard University — that is where the real power in America lies, and it is the rejection of those institutions and symbols that distinguishes radicals. That is not to say that I love the *Daily News* but that I consider it more honest than the New York *Times*. I once wanted to start a newspaper called the New York *Liar*. It would be the most honest paper in the country. I would sit in a dark closet and write all the news. The paper would be printed with lemon juice, which is invisible until you heat it with an iron, hence involving the reader. I would write about events without ever leaving the closet. The point is, we all live in dark closets. We all see things through a closet darkly.

That's some fantasy.
Of course. It'll come true, though. Fantasy is the only truth.
Once we had a demonstration at the *Daily News* Building.
About three hundred people smoked pot, danced, sprayed the
reporters with body deodorant, burned money, handed out
leaflets to all the employees that began: "Dear fellow member
of the Communist conspiracy. . . ." We called it an "Alternative
Fantasy." It worked great.

What do you mean, it worked great?
Nobody understood it. That is, nobody could explain what it all
meant yet everyone was fascinated. It was pure information,
pure imagery, which in the end is truth. You see, the New York
Times can get into very theoretical discussions on the critical
level of what we are doing. The *Daily News* responds on a gut
level. That's it. The New York *Times* has no guts.

Then being understood is not your goal?
Of course not. The only way you can understand is to join, to
become involved. Our goal is to remain a mystery. Pure theater.
Free, with no boundaries except your own. Throwing money
onto the floor of the Stock Exchange is pure information. It
needs no explanation. It says more than thousands of anti-
capitalist tracts and essays. It's so obvious that I hesitate to discuss it, since everyone reading this already has an image of
what happened there. I respect their images. Anything I said
would come on like expertise. "Now, this is what *really* happened." In point of fact nothing happened. Neither we nor the
Stock Exchange exist. We are both rumors. That's it. That's
what happened that day. Two different rumors collided.

Can you think of any people in theater that influence you?
W. C. Fields, Ernie Kovacs, Ché Guevara, Antonin Artaud,
Alfred Hitchcock, Lenny Bruce, the Marx Brothers — probably
the Beatles have the most influence. I think they have the perfect model for the new family. They have unlimited creativity.

They are a continual process, always changing, always burying
the old Beatles, always dropping out.

Can you pursue that a little?
Well, the Beatles are a new family group. They are organized
around the way they create. They are communal art. They are
brothers and, along with their wives and girl friends, form a
family unit that is horizontal rather than vertical, in that it ex-
tends across a peer group rather than descending vertically like
grandparents–parents–children. More than horizontal, it's cir-
cular with the four Beatles the inner circle, then their wives and
kids and friends. The Beatles are a small circle of friends, a
tribe. They are far more than simply a musical band. Let's say,
if you want to begin to understand our culture, you can start
by comparing Frank Sinatra and the Beatles. It wouldn't be
perfect but it would be a good beginning. Music is always a
good place to start.

Why is that?
Well, a revolution always has rhythm. Whether it's songs of the
Lincoln Brigade, black soul music, Cuban love songs by José
Martí, or white psychedelic rock. I once heard songs of the
Algerian rebels that consisted mostly of people beating guns on
wooden cases. It was fantastic. What is the music of the system?
Kate Smith singing the National Anthem. Maybe that's Camp,
but it's not Soul.

What about dancing?
There too. Arthur Murray. Dance lessons. What a joke. If you
need lessons you haven't got the message. Dancing for us is
doing anything you want. You have to see a huge throbbing
light-rock show. Especially one that is free, because the free-est
people only go to free events. You will see people doing all sorts
of fantastic dances. Frenzied and smooth. Butterflies and ante-
lopes. Indians and spiders. Swimming and jumping. Lots of
people just sit or lie on the floor, which is a nice step too. No-

body takes lessons. In fact, if you liked the way somebody danced and asked them where they learned to do it, they would laugh. Dance schools are about as outmoded as public schools, which really are archaic. In fact, I wouldn't be surprised to find out that Arthur Murray was U.S. Commissioner of Education, and high school was just a training ground for millions of fox-trotters. You can see the difference if you look at one of those silly dance books with the shoe prints. One-Two-Three, One-Two-Three. You know. It would be funny to make one for the new dances, which, by the way, don't have names anymore. I think about two years ago dances stopped having names. Anyway, one of those books would have shoe-prints all over the walls and ceilings. A possible title for this book I'm working on could be *The Three Basic Steps in Modern Dance*. One—Two—FREE . . . One—Three—T . . . O . . . net wo . . . 10—9—8—7—6—5—4—3—2—1 NOW! That's it. Now you've got it. Turn your motor on and fly. You can go forever.

Forever?
Haven't you heard of nuclear energy? Yes, you can dance forever. That's the Beatles' message. That's why I said before that our movement was called Dancing.

Doesn't all this dancing present a problem for society?
Not for ours, but for the parent culture, the one decaying, most definitely. The cops hate us.

How do you feel about cops?
Cops are our enemy. Not each one as a person, naked, say. We're all brothers when we are naked. Did you ever see a fight in a steam bath? But cops in uniform are a different story. Actually, all uniforms are enemies. Just another extension of machine living. The way we dress — in costumes — is in direct opposition to a uniform culture. Costumes are the opposite of uniforms. Since the cops' uniforms also include clubs, handcuffs, guns, etc., they are particularly hated uniforms. I should also

add that I've been arrested seventeen times and beaten by
police on at least five occasions. I would no more think of asking
a cop for help than shooting arsenic to get high.

Who would you ask for help?
My brothers. None of my brothers are cops. You see a cop's
principal role is to protect private property. Our goal is the
abolition of property. How could I ever call a cop?

Don't they do more than protect property?
Yeah, they kick the shit out of people who have none. Listen.
You should have seen Grand Central Station last week during the
YIP-IN. Picture this, thousands, maybe ten thousand people,
dancing, singing, throwing balloons in the air. Some people
decided to climb on top of the information booth; while they
were up there they pulled the hands off the clock. This triggered
a police riot, with maybe two hundred cops swinging night-
sticks charging into people. No warning. No order to clear.
About one hundred people were hospitalized, including my wife
and me, and over sixty people arrested. There were the police
lined up around the clock, guarding it while others smashed
skulls. One kid, Ron Shea, tried to come to my rescue while I
was being beaten. He was thrown through a glass door and had
both hands broken. He may never be able to use one again.
Which hands do you think the cops cared more about, the
hands on the clock or Ron Shea's hands?

Why did the kids rip the hands off the clock?
I don't know. Maybe they hate time and schedules. Maybe they
thought the clock was ugly. They also decorated the clock with
sketches. Maybe they were having fun. When we put on a large
celebration the aim is to create a liberated area. People can do
whatever they want. They can begin to live the revolution even
if only within a confined area. We will learn how to govern
ourselves. By the way, this goes on in every revolution. Take
Vietnam. In liberated zones the National Liberation Front has

schools and theater troupes and hospitals and building programs.
The revolutionary experience is far more than just the fighting
units.

Do you read revolutionary writings?
Yes, Guevara, Debray, Mao, Giap, McLuhan. I find Giap and
McLuhan the most interesting. But of course I am totally caught
up with Ché as a hero. His death moved me far more than, say,
that of Martin Luther King. Although King's was a shock also.

What do you think of death?
Well, I must say I have no fear of death. I faced it once about
two years ago on an internal level. This is hard to explain. I've
actually faced the risk of death a number of times but this one
time I actually became paranoid. I was overcome with anxiety.
It was unclear what was going on. I overcame that state purely
on a mind level and realized that I had the power in me not to
become paranoid. It's the paranoia, the living in constant fear
of death, that is the real bad trip, not the death itself. I will be
surprised if I get a chance to live out my life. Gleefully surprised, but surprised none the less.

Isn't that sort of gloomy?
No! Not really. You can't deny there is a tremendous amount of
violence in this country. People who are engaged daily in radical social change are always exposed to that violence. I would
rather die fighting for change than surrender. Death in a physical sense is just not seen as the worst of all possible things.

What is?
I don't know. Going to jail. Surrendering. . . . Maybe nothing
is really bad, since I am so convinced that we will win the
future.

THE WHITE NIGGERS

You want to get a glimpse of what it feels like to be a nigger? Let your hair grow long. Longhairs, that new minority, are getting the crap kicked out of them by cops all over the country, and with the beatings and jailings comes the destruction of flower power. Cops EAT FLOWERS painted in large white letters last fall on Second Avenue and St. Marks Place signaled the end of flower power. As the kids pour back into the Lower East Side they bring with them tales of police harassment previously reserved only for blacks. Two hundred kids busted on Boston Common for "idleness." Three kids arrested for vagrancy in Nevada (even though they all had money) and held fifty days before they even had a trial. Kids arrested in Indiana get their hair cut and then are thrown out of the jail without even going to trial. In Florida a head shop was smashed by the police and the owners were told bluntly, "We don't want your kind around here. Get your ass out of town." Anyone who takes to the road going cross-country literally takes his life in his hands.

Here in enlightened New York things are not much better. The block I live on, St. Marks Place, is patrolled by no less than twenty cops at a time (one block!). Undercover agents in plain clothes slouch against the building waiting for trouble. Kids being searched and asked to produce identification is a normal occurrence. Communes are raided by the week in a massive hunt for America's young runaways.

Pot, long used as a method of busting black people, is now being used as a means of eliminating young white activists. There are, I am told, over thirty thousand people currently in prison for smoking pot. On the Lower East Side pot is more common than cigarettes. Public Smoke-Ins in Tompkins Square Park last summer attracted five thousand heads each time. The police had just about thrown in the towel and concentrated on eliminating major dealers (which is difficult since, by definition, a major dealer has already bribed the cops). That was true at least up until a month ago. Jerry Rubin is a well known activist on the Lower East Side. A confirmed radical, Jerry was active in the Berkeley Free Speech Movement, the Vietnam Day Committee, project director of October's seige at the Pentagon, a key figure in Yippie! and an architect of plans for demonstrations at the Democratic National Convention in Chicago. Detectives from the Narcotics Squad raided his apartment, ripped a poster of Castro off the wall, searched his files and phone book for information, and forced him up against the wall, demanding information on Yippie! plans for Chicago. All this was under the pretext of a pot bust. The pot, however, was not as interesting to the cops as Jerry's politics, and for not talking Jerry received a few slugs and a kick in the back which resulted in a fractured coccyx. Jerry is on trial now and could receive up to fifteen years in prison for something which I'm sure we all do, namely take a puff on a harmless flower. A simple weed that grows wild and has been used by people for thousands of years seems to be causing some fuss.

I have no friend who has not been in jail. Jail for even one night can be a learning experience equal to a year in college. Did you know, for example, that you can commit suicide by stuffing cigarette filters in your mouth? Only cops could think that one up. Filters are cut off all your cigarettes in jail. Did you ever have your ass searched? I always wonder what they are looking for. Machine guns? Supreme Court decisions? Civil rights? The Supreme Court is a long way from the Ninth Precinct and the Ninth Precinct is a longer way still from the cop on the beat.

People down here are arrested for passing out leaflets, standing on the corner, handing out free food, not carrying identification, and a variety of similar offenses. Recently six armed cops arrested a longhair on charges of conspiracy. It was never explained how one person can commit conspiracy. All these cases are now being thrown out of the courts by puzzled judges, but looking out the window on St. Marks Place one wonders how long it will take before people will be put away for long terms in prison for such activities. Paranoids are prophets down here.

I was recently busted for standing on the corner of my block. In the police station a TPF (Tactical Patrol Force) cop threatened to gouge my eyes out with his fingers if I didn't stop smiling. He had assured me he was proficient at such tasks. He gave me a punch in the head just to let me know he knew some other tricks besides eye-gouging. It is this reality we are bringing to Chicago with us — the reality of our daily lives.

RUNAWAYS: THE SLAVE REVOLT

About eight months ago I was picking my way through the garbage-strewn streets between Avenues B and C when a mite of a girl bumped into me. She must have been about thirteen or so and was off to St. Marks Place to practice her trade. She was a panhandler. She was barefoot, her dungarees were at least three sizes too big, and her long yellow hair was tangled in the silver beads she had around her neck. We struck up a conversation. She was from Ohio; she had been down here three weeks and found the going tough. After about fifteen minutes of listening to problems like "finding a decent crash pad . . . the number of times you get burned down here . . . my parents got me on a permanent paranoid trip" and the like, I suggested, "Why don't you go home?" She got very indignant. Assuming a pose even Bonnie Parker would have dug, she pointed her finger in my face and spat out, "WHY DON'T YOU!"

I went to school on that. It was the last time I ever considered it an alternative for anyone. Runaways are the backbone of the youth revolution. We are all runaways, age is irrelevant. A fifteen-year-old kid who takes off from middle-class American life is an escaped slave crossing the Mason-Dixon line. They are hunted down by professional bounty hunters, fidgety relatives and the law, because it is against the law to leave home (translate: bondage) until you have finished your servitude. Many a stool has been known for turning in a known runaway when the reward became big enough. One media legend "hippie" made a practice out of using his free crash pad as a trap for runaways newly arrived on the scene. It's a fast-growing business, and with the runaway figure for the United States up 18 percent from a year ago, it looks like its future is assured.

It's really quite interesting to stand on the corner of Avenue A and 10th Street and watch the scores of relatives with puzzled expressions on their faces, scurrying to and fro. Here and there is a bounty hunter or plainclothesman querying the local gossips. The parents are really a sight, plowing through incense-burning, rock-blasting psychedelic shops, "Please, Mary, won't you come home; we all love you." About two sets of parents a week make their way to my apartment. Somehow I have this reputation for being "in the know." They are referred by the police or shopkeepers. We talk a little. Sometimes I get personal. "What drugs was she using?" "Oh, Janie would never think of taking drugs." There never was a parent who believes his kid uses drugs and I've never met a kid in the Lower East Side who didn't use drugs before he got here. It seems America has a failure of communication going. **It seems America has lost her children.** They come down here or to Haight-Ashbury or to the stops in between. An underground railroad exists. The runaways are hidden in crash pads, communes, apartments, in country communities. They let their hair grow, change their style of dress, and vanish. The pictures that are stuck on police-station walls, printed in underground newspapers, or thrown in my wastebasket, are of different people. A nice school photo. Girl with lipstick, pert dress with white collar. Boy with tweedy sportsjacket, windsor knot in his tie, hair parted on the right side. Where have all the neckties gone? Are the runaways going back? I don't know. Ask them. I'll tell you one thing — I sure as hell ain't, they'll have to kill me first.

CALM
BEFORE THE
STORM

It's a sunny day on the Boston Common. Couples lie on the grass, the swan boats flutter in the pond, kids playing Frisbee and catch. One big happy scene. America the Beautiful. You can snap a neat Kodachrome in your mind and send it all over the world. A young girl with long hair, beads, and sandals winks at you and hands you a leaflet. "Last night on the Boston Common the cops smashed our Be-in. They brought out the dogs. They clubbed and tear-gassed us and arrested 65. Tonight we assemble again. Don't let the pigs take our park. . . . The streets belong to the people."

The girl moves on, handing out the leaflets in a very selective manner that looks ever so casual. A leaflet to a black couple. One hesitatingly for the Frisbee players. A leaflet and a hug for two longhair guys, one playing a flute. About a fourth of the people in the area got leaflets. Comrades being gathered for the Second American Revolution. No leaflets for the Tories. The girl had ripped the Kodachrome in two. The eyes blinked and one saw two pictures. THEM—US. And then more . . .

muskets, redcoats and freedom rides, bells, blue-noses, FUCK
... naked bodies in the pool ... statues all moldy ... state capital on the hill ... and childhood reminiscence, for Boston was
home. The girl and the two longhair guys are transformed,
they are Crispus Attucks, they are kneeling praying in a Bir-
mingham church when a bomb comes flying through the window. A heavy voice from behind me smirks up out of the leaflet
and drawls, "Hey, boy, you people better not start anything
tonight, we don't like your kind in Boston." Yassuh, it was
coon huntin' season all over again. The United States of Mississippi had found themselves another nigger.

July 21, 1968

4

YIPPIE! – THE MEDIA MYTH

BLANK SPACE AS COMMUNICATION

It is a preview. Have you ever noticed how movie previews are done? They are done by the best minds in Hollywood. TV ads, as of lately, have the same effectiveness. They create a dynamism. The viewer becomes involved. Expectations are built up. Needs are addressed. They are totally absorbing with all the quick cuts, slogans, flashing images and exciting tempos. Movie previews and TV ads are written by our modern poets. They know how to create the blank space into which the viewer can place himself. Television is more like swimming than reading books.

All movie previews are rumors. They all exaggerate. "The greatest movie in twenty years!" Fireworks explode. Wow! "Don't miss this one." Zoom. "Bare-backed girl." Flash. "Exposed." Everything spins. Eight scenes compressed in five-second flashes.

TV ads are also rumors. They are not always hot as the image of the movie preview. Some are cool. Cool images promote security. They typify banks, insurance companies, airlines, government agencies. A typical one is the ad for the Dreyfus Fund. A lion walks unnoticed down Wall Street. Slump. Slump. Slump. Strong, determined, with a sense of the future. You are the lion amid the sterile world around you. Where are you going? The lion jumps onto the word "Dreyfus." "*Growl.*" He is satisfied. "INVEST IN DREYFUS." Few words are needed. Words confuse. Words are hot. A lion in a street of people is worth a thousand words. It is a wonderful ad, fantastically filmed. A lion walking in a crowded street is totally absorbing. There is

an underlying tension of course, but overall coolness. No chaos.
No anarchy. No risks. Just give us your dough. Maybe we
should run a lion for President?

Projecting cool images is not our goal. We do not wish to
project a calm secure future. We are disruption. We are hot.
In our ad the lion cracks. Races through the streets. We are
cannibals, cowboys, Indians, witches, warlocks. Weird-looking
freaks that crawl out of the cracks in America's nightmare.
Very visible and, as everyone knows, straight from the white
middle-class suburban life. We are a pain in the ass to America
because we cannot be explained. Blacks riot because they are
oppressed. An Italian cabdriver told me, "If I was black, I'd be
pissed, too." America understands the blacks.

We are alienated. What's that all about? Existential lovers in
a plastic society. Our very existence is disruptive. Long hair
and freaky clothes are total information. It is not necessary to
say we are opposed to the ———. Everybody already knows.
It is a mistake to tell people what they already know. We
alienate people. We involve people. Attract–Repel. We play
on the generation gap. Parents shit. They are baffled, confused.
They want the cool lion. We tear through the streets. Kids love
it. They understand it on an internal level. We are living TV
ads, movies. Yippie! There is no program. Program would make
our movement sterile. We are living contradictions. I cannot
really explain it. I do not even understand it myself.

Blank space, the interrupted statement, the unsolved puzzle,
they are all involving. There is a classic experiment in psychology. Subjects are given problems to solve. Some tasks they complete; others are interrupted. Six months later they are given a
memory test. They consistently remember the problems that
were interrupted. Let's postulate a third setting, in which the
subject is shown how to solve the problem by an instructor. It
would probably be the least remembered of the three. It is
called "going to school" and is the least involving relationship.

When we opened the FREE STORE we circulated a leaflet with
a beautiful work of art, and under it in Spanish was the line:

Everything is free at the store of the Diggers. No address. No store hours. No list of items and services. It was tremendously effective. Puerto Ricans began asking questions. Puerto Ricans talked to hippies. Everybody searched for the FREE STORE together.

I stare at a button. Bright pink on purple background: Yippie! It pops right out. It's mispelled. Good. Misspelling can be a creative act. What does Yippie! mean? Energy — excitement — fun — fierceness — exclamation point! Last December three of us sat in a room discussing plans to bring people to Chicago to make a statement about the Democratic Convention. Hippies are dead. Youth International Party — Y.I.P. — YIP — YIPPIE!. We're all jumping around the room, Paul Krassner, Jerry Rubin, and I. Playing Yippie! games. "Y." "Right." That's our symbol. That's our question. "Join the Y." "God, Nixon will attack us in three months for confusing the image of the YMCA." Within fifteen minutes we have created a myth. Head for the media. "Hello, my name is Paul Yippie, what's yours!" Within two weeks every underground paper has a Yippie! story. In a month *Newsweek* writes "the Yippies Are Coming." Lawrence Lipton, in the L.A. *Free Press*, analyzes Yippie! origins. Y's appear magically on walls around the country. All the while, the excitement and energy are focused on Chicago and people get involved. A Yippie! button produces a question. The wearer must answer. He tells a little story. He mentions Chicago, a festival of music, violence (Americans love to go to accidents and fires), guerrilla theater, Democrats. Each story is told in a different way. There is mass participation in the Yippie! myth. Can we change an H to a Y? Can myths involve people to the extent that they will make the journey to far-off Chicago? Can magic media succeed where organizing has failed? Y not?

Blank space is the transmission of information whereby the viewer has an opportunity to become involved as a participant.

In Saigon, the newspapers are censored. Various pages have sections of blank news articles. There is more information in those blank articles than you might suspect. I go on television and make a point of swearing. I know the little fuckers don't get through, but the image of me blabbing away with the enthusiasm and excitement of a future world better than this while being sliced up by the puritanical, sterile culture of the Establishment is information worth conveying.
Words
        can
            be
                used
                    to
                        create
                            •

TV TRIP AFTER KING GOT IT

Whitney Young is obviously alive and well in America. I see him every two minutes on Channel Control. And there is Johnson. Wow. Look at him, saggy old LBJ calling for nonviolence. Funny, General Waste-more-land didn't mention sit-ins in the Mekong Delta as part of the Army's new tactics. It's funny to see panel shows on "Where do we go from here?" and know the country is burning down.

Marty walks to the corner and pulls the fire alarm. Within minutes the fire engines have arrived and Marty, sitting on the curb licking a butter-almond cone from Gem Spa, looks up and says "The country is burning." They slap the kid and call the cops who take him to Bellevue.

"Where the hell is Eldridge Cleaver?" Someone High-Up obviously decided the guy was too hot on the same Sunday that he gets shot by an asshole cop in Oakland. Too bad. David Susskind won't let Eldridge on to do his thing. There are limits to freedom of speech. On a snowy night in December you can go on the telly and yell Burn, Baby, Burn, but not this Sunday night as you lie wounded in San Quentin Penitentiary. So instead we get Percy Sutton and argue whether or not he's white or black or gay or toupeed.

An old friend, a priest, calls drunk and crying and blurting out lines from "We Shall Overcome," saying we gotta go to Memphis, like the old days and I tell him I ain't marching anymore and especially not with George Meany. He asks what he should do and I tell him to fuck a nun. "Hey, LBJ's on, come on in!" I hang up on my old friend, singing "This little light of mine, I'm gonna let it shine" . . . click! Oh, is that what that song meant, I wonder as Washington burns in the living room. "Becauseofratherunusualcircumstancesthecherryblossomfestivalhasbeencancelled . . . Touristsarebeingmetatthegates andadvisedtovisitArlingtonVirginiaormaybegobacktoWilliamsburg . . ."

"Gee, Mary, I know we've come all this way to see the cherry blossoms and the Capitol, but the troops say it's too dangerous."

"Can we go back to Baltimore?"

"No, they say there are 4,000 troops there now and more due in."

"The kids are getting cranky, Marvin, what are we going to do? We can't go back to Pittsburgh, that's a mess."

"I can't understand why they don't shoot all those niggers."

"Frank, that's not nice to say, especially not so soon after King got killed."

The nice family spent the night at a Howard Johnson's and the next day drove into the city.

"Let's go to the Memorial Service, I hear Jacqueline Kennedy's going to be there."

"We might as well. It would be awful to have come all this way for nothing."

THE NIGHT THE RED SOX
ATTACKED THE U.S. EMBASSY

TV images flash in my head. Vietnam news pictured in terms of old World War II movies and they are not the Japanese but tiny bands of underdog heroes like beautiful Filipinos I once saw sabotage Japanese Military Might in surprise attack and now nineteen Vietcong guerrillas on heroic mission attack the U.S. Embassy when they said it couldn't be done. Who would have believed that crew-cut generals in shiny limousines and million-dollar planes that zoom by, dropping latest university developments brewed by those institutions we were taught as children to awe, could be whipped by nineteen gooks? America will lose more than its face in Vietnam rice paddies hunting jackknife warriors with napalm machines. Where will be our Alamos? Where even our brave men planting flag on Iwo Jima hilltop? America is a mythic land. Dreamed up by European beatniks, religious fanatics, draft dodgers, assorted hippie kooks, and runaways from servitude off to the New World of milk and honey. Europe said, "If you don't like it here, why don't you leave." Echoed three hundred years later by a middle-aged veteran with sagging ass and sagging belly hunched over sign reading IF YOUR HEART IS NOT IN AMERICA GET YOUR ASS OUT. Sagging crudeness of Joe McCarthy national policy. And even as we slaughtered the Indians, as children we could accept the encircled group of covered wagons fighting to defend themselves and wanting simply to make it to a little pastureland in the green hills and valleys of California.

The myths of America are strong and good but the institutional machine is a trap of death. Can you believe I was eighteen before I even knew this country had a Depression but at thirteen I could list with correct dates all Revolutionary War battles and discuss in detail the battle at Lexington and Concord which took place just thirty miles from my hometown? *Just last summer I stood on that bridge at 6 A.M. with a follower of trancendental meditation and described the battle, joining myself with imaginary musket to the ragged guerrillas that shot from those peaceful hills in Concord on that April morning. The previous day we had stood in Harvard Square passing out free poems hurling curses at the Pentagon gone mad and were attacked by drunk Marines as Harvard fairy professors stood in a circle of Adlai Stevenson-nothingness and watched and appealed to His Majesty's protectors of law and order, who finally did something. They took down our names and told us to get our asses out of Cambridge. I came away from sitting on the Concord Bridge that night knowing that some day I might just have to shoot a few of His Majesty's gendarmes and forgetting those nights of practicing how to protect my head and nuts in pacifist utero position and believing in the Second American Revolution.* America lost its balls in the frontier and since then there have been no mighty myths and now we hunt for them in lonely balconies, watching *Bonnie and Clyde*. Tragic figures, born out of rejection of a machine-mad American sterility, like James Dean and Marilyn Monroe crushed by plastic Hollywood. And later through a drugged comedian named Lenny, who had more balls by far than the stream of district attorneys that chased him with outmoded statutes.

Now I can write FUCK and nobody's prurient interests stir and no one gets upset except maybe the DAR, which is so drugged on *The Sound of Music* that it only dreams in paranoid fantasies that such words are written, not to even mention the fact that the daughters of the Daughters are getting fucked all the time even if they are just panty raids. There are other heroes also, not home-grown, for the bowels of corporate success do not easily give birth to champions like Fidel. *I remember in the winter of '59 as we thousands cheered Fidel in Harvard Stadium as we had on New Year's day (even if he did interrupt the Rose Bowl game), Julius Lester told me of a trip he was on with him in the Cuban countryside. When the helicopter landed with the newspapers from Havana, Fidel quickly turned to the baseball scores and then threw the paper into the trash barrel. Cuba Si, Yankee No. Up in Boston we would yell the same sort of thing from the bleachers in Fenway Park. How the hell would anybody ever beat the Yankees?*

The Cubans finally did and last year so did the Red Sox. Even New Yorkers now abandon the old beaten men of the Yankees and root for the Mets. In those days of Yankee might we would go out to Fenway Park just to see Jim Piersall sit down in the middle of the game or get in a fight with the umpire. All the umpires secretly worked for the Yankees. Jim Piersall lives and so does the Revolution! *Venceremos!* Up against the wall, Mickey Mantle!

APRIL 11, 2001

The only pure revolution in the end is technology. Yet that is the same as the revolution in consciousness. Funny, one thing

just buttons, light bulbs, needles and thread. The other totally
internal, spiritual, personal, emotional — *al* (do all those words
end in *al* or is that just individual). It is in the fusion of that
and endless other dichotomies that the road to revolution lies.
The movie CINERAMA ——— *2001* ——— on LSD (but is that
also an illusion?) is a Revolutionary breakthrough. Not that other
movies (some good, some bad) do not have things to say, but
2001 has things to feel in it and it's fascinating how all the
human emotions, joy, sadness, love, anxiety, jealousy, hatred,
on and on, come through so clearly in a film that on its surface
seems to deal so much with machines and the mastery of them.
I mean, where the fuck are the tits and ass that we have been
conditioned to see as dealing with the emotional side of man?
Where is the blood? Where is the pain? No, *2001* takes us
beyond all that earthly stuff and truly gives us a glimpse of the
future.

The future, where is that? Someone rips a ticket in half,
guides you to a plush chair, the light dims and soon, soon you
are out there. In fact ,   at times w a y   out there,
2 0 0 1 beyond, nearthespeedoflight, you realize theFutureis:
Broadway, flashing lights, sootyair, cars c r u n c h i n g
from brakes that need lubrication, abeggarasksforanickel —
andyourealize theFutureis N O W !   *2001* is the apex of
technological communication this civilization has reached; of
course when you are suspended one might say a flower contains all one needs to know.

Today was a typical day. Today everything happened. The
moon is full, an Aries moon, I'm told by revolutionary astrolo-
gers, and in three days the YIP-Out and thousands upon
thousands will gather together in Central Park and meet each
other and smile and some will ask why they are there and
others will know. Some will tell others. Others will nod. Skep-
tics meet true believers. Left meets Right. Mao Tse-tung of
the People's Republic of China will bump into Cousin Clyde of
the Hell's Angels. "Let a thousand flowers bloom" meets "I
jes' like to blow minds." A Be-In is an emotional United Na-

tions. It works where the intellectual one ten blocks to the east enclosed in glass and concrete fails . . .

Today I asked Joel, the perpetual runaway, scared kid, to go and buy three flowers: one chrysanthemum, one daffodil, and one daisy — and he did and returned with the change. We had a technological problem. Which flowers would be best suited to throw out of an airplane into the YIP-Out? This was a problem, if you had visions of 10,000 stems *sans* blossoms descending on 50,000 bewildered heads. So up the twelve flights of stairs I trudged, three flowers in hand, exhausted, puffing, out of breath as if I had climbed the Himalayas (which I had in fact done). Up on the roof the sun shone brightly, pigeons were flying about. To the right lay the street, with dutiful Joel waiting to see which flower stood up the best.

There were two men on the roof. Two old men, one in his late forties, the other about sixty-five. Old Italian men with old ways and old hats feeding pigeons, hundreds of them. It was their thing. "You can't come up here" one started screaming. It was weird, they started yelling all kinds of shit like "the landlord said . . ." and "you can't come here . . ." and calling me all kinds of names "You people . . ." and I got mad and started yelling things like "I live in this fuckin' building, what do you mean 'you people' . . ." And there they were defending their territory, birds, governments, who knows what . . . We did not speak the same language and one old man ran into a little wooden shed on the roof and came out with a butcher knife and the younger one restrained me as I stood with three flowers raised over my head ready to attack and after we had all shouted I went down the stairs and there was Joel staring upward and I said, "Joel, we'll try it from across the street." I climbed six flights to the roof of the Electric Circus, signaled to Joel, and threw the flowers down. First the chrysanthemum, then the daffodil, and finally the white daisy. Klunch, klunch, klunch. Each hit the sidewalk intact. I ran down the stairs and Joel, puffing, met me halfway and said "A kid stole the chrysanthemum and somebody stepped on the daffodil." He was

clutching a white daisy in both hands. He was smiling. The
Scientific Method leads to Joy. Daisies would make it to the
YIP-Out.

That wasn't all that happened today. Today Anita and I
applied for passports. Just in case. That wasn't all either. Today
was 10,000 years wide.

GETTING IT ALL OUT THERE (1)

America is Racist.
America is Imperialistic.
Police are Brutal.
Mass media distort.
Bah — Bah — Bah — Bah — Bah — Bah — Bah — Bah — Bah
Sheep talking rhetoric. People on the Left spend most of their
time telling each other things like that. The point is, everybody
already knows, so call it Rhetoric. The Left masturbates con-
tinuously because it is essentially rooted in an academic tradition.* It is the rhetoric of the Left, its insistence on ideological
exactness rather than action, that has held the revolution back
in this country as much as the actions of the people in power.
The Left has the same smugness as the New York *Times*. I
remember about four months ago attending a Mobilization
meeting as part of Yippie! They did not want to include us in
their coalition because they said we had no real constituency.
We didn't even request to be included and made a point of

* This, of course, wasn't true of the left movement in the thirties,
when it was rooted in the labor movement. Dock workers don't waste
time at conferences and ideological debates. They were also ready to
use any means necessary ... that's how they got what they wanted.

asking them not to support us. We just wanted to let people know we would be there. For two days the MOB debated whether or not they should go to Chicago in August. We laughed at them but not in a hostile way, sort of like Buddhas smiling in the corner. While they argued back and forth we got stoned, made love to all the pretty girls, offered resolutions, like demanding an end to pay toilets and support of the Polish student rebellion (just to upset the Russian-linked U.S. Communist Party), refused to pay for our meals, and in general carried on like bad, crazy niggers. After two days of bullshit they postponed a decision until sometime in July. We came into the hall and passed out huge posters (a picture of the U.S.A. as a jigsaw puzzle all mixed up with an arrow saying Yippie! pointing to Chicago. It said Festival of Life, Chicago, August 25–30 – Lights-Theater-Magic-Free-Music). We gave everyone a Yippie! button. All free of course. Then we left, knowing full well they'd all be in Chicago anyway. There was no point meeting with them again and we didn't. No Constituency! HA! The five of us° represented the most important underground magazine, the two most important figures on the N.Y. Hippie Scene, the most important movement radio personality, and the hero of the Pentagon (see Mailer's *Armies of the Night*). We had on our team the most dynamic people in the white drop-out movement: Leary, Ginsberg, and more importantly the rock musicians and most of the underground editors, especially Liberation News Service, the most exciting figures in guerrilla theater as well as the most original people on Broadway, and even more. Essentially what we had was information control, tremendous ability to manipulate the media, and enough balls to break every rule in the book. We could act like Buddhas, we had in six weeks already told the whole world we were going to the Democratic Convention. The night before we had come from the Grand Central Station Massacre of the Yippies.

In one week, on fifteen dollars cash, we had attracted five to

° Myself, Jim Fouratt, Paul Krassner, Jerry Rubin, and Bob Fass.

eight thousand people to a party at midnight, for no reason, in Grand Central Station. It is debatable whether or not the Grand Central Massacre helped or hurt our chances in Chicago. I maintain it helped tremendously. It put Yippie! on the map. I know that sounds cold-blooded. Revolutionists are cold-blooded bastards (the best are also good lovers). I can say this honestly because I run the same, if not more risks, than any-one. I was knocked unconscious by some dumb pig in Grand Central; besides, nobody was under orders to come. (Only people in business really manipulate people because they have money-power and, as everyone knows, money IS power in America.) Besides, I was the only one who tried to cool out the scene. I asked the head cops and the Mayor's assistant, Barry Gottehrer to let me use the P.A. system. Like dumb cops they refused, in fact they refused even to use it themselves. The Mayor's assistant had an interesting response. "They are not our police," he replied. Asking to use the P.A. system was a very difficult decision which very few people in this country can even begin to comprehend. It means a conscious, delib-erate attempt to assert leadership. It's nice in a sense that the cops, as they did later in Chicago, always take over the leader-ship at such critical moments. "The pigs are our leaders" is the kind of information that is truer than true.

Anyway, a revolutionary artist, which is shorthand for either Revolutionist or Artist, just does it. Life-actors, all play their roles according to their backgrounds, talents, costumes, and props. The Grand Central Station Massacre knocked out the hippie image of Chicago and let the whole world know there would be blood on the streets of Chicago. It didn't matter what we predicted, what story we made up, how much we talked of fun and games. The medium is the message and the message was Theater of Cruelty. The rumor of Grand Central Station and the statements of Shoot-to-Kill Daley and Sheriff Joe Woods ("We'll stick them in underground mud tunnels and or-ganize white vigilante groups") were powerful enough magic to separate the hippies from the Yippies.

No one who came to Chicago because of our influence had any doubts that they were risking their life. I don't know about McCarthy kids; to use a Mother term, they were not our "responsibility." The hippie end of our mythical coalition dropped out. They failed to trust the Yippie! myth. There was a lot of name-calling but in the end it didn't matter; almost all the original hippies could be found on the streets of Chicago and they were all fighting in the style of their choice, all stoned out of their heads and all having a ball. The reason for this is that the energy centers that gravitated to the center of the myth were tough as all hell. Also a myth has a tendency to always pick the right symbols and strategy, it is in a real sense self-perpetuating.

For example, we held only one formal press conference until Chicago actually happened. It was arranged by one of the country's best publicists, held in the Americana Hotel (which of course we got FREE) and only the stars spoke, Ginsberg, Judy Collins, Phil Ochs, Jacques Levy (Broadway director), Joe Byrd (head of U.S.A. band), Al Cooper (Blood, Sweat & Tears), Bob Fass (WBAI-FM), Michael Goldstein (top P.R. man in the rock field), Paul Krassner, and Ed Sanders. Jerry Rubin and I did not speak. Except for Paul and Ed, all the others later dropped out of Yippie! until the Festival began. Some played secondary roles, not the least of which was to criticize Yippie! Maybe for this reason the press conference got very little coverage in the media? Maybe it was because of the Americana setting, maybe because of other news that day? By the rules, this press conference should have gotten into every paper in the country and on every TV station. It didn't, and it didn't precisely because it wasn't right. It didn't fit the truth of what would happen in Chicago. The media in a real sense never lie when you relate to them in a non-linear mythical manner. In similar fashion the YIP-Out on Easter Sunday, with over 40,000 people in Central Park and fifteen rock groups and flowers from the sky, didn't fit the myth (as well as being a lousy spectator event) and was soon forgotten. It was Grand Central Station that stuck, and talk of not telling the truth is pigshit for a myth always tells the truth.

Another case in point is the Pig. Introduced fairly early in the game by Hugh Romney, spiritual leader of the Hogfarm, a commune outside Los Angeles, the Pig gravitated to the center of the myth. It took a long time, probably because of Hugh's vacillation about coming, and the fact that he was bringing the Pig probably held the myth back.° During the week before the thing happened we noticed the media picking up on the Pig; with the cold-bloodedness of Madison Avenue we rammed in the Pigshit. It took only four days. When I went out to get the Pig on some American farm in Northern Illinois,°° the Pig had already become famous.

This particular pig was finally rejected by the myth — with a good deal of help from Jerry Rubin and Stu Albert. The meeting at which this decision was made was quite heated and actually our only "meeting" in Chicago. They wanted a meaner pig. I thought it didn't matter, sort of liked the pig we had, was worried about the technical problems of managing a large pig, and had doubts that Jerry, Stu, and Phil Ochs could find another pig in time. They were not the resource people, who were all in my gang by that time. Jerry°°° and I had a huge fight and didn't speak to each other the rest of the time. Which upset everybody except probably Jerry and me, since we were both so determined to make our Chicago in our own style. We would not let a personal fight upset anything. Besides, we were both so dedicated that I, at least, realized that Jerry would cry at my funeral and make the right speech and that I would do

° Hugh never made it to Chicago, even though when it started he called, saying he would be there with his traveling show in a day if we could wire him $500, which, of course, we couldn't and would not even if we'd had the money.

°° Speaking of coincidences, the farm where we got Mrs. Pig was in Belvidere, Illinois, home of the current Miss America.

°°° I even remember Jerry remarking ten days before we entered Lincoln Park that the Money Burning was our best bit. As it turned out, we didn't stage the Money Burning. I can remember burning only one dollar in Chicago. Did anybody burn any dollars? We had no money at all. Even our half of the benefit with the Mob on Tuesday night we gave to them. I don't think we know what to do with money.

the same at his. But I deliberately told my police tail and everyone else except the reporters about the fight we had. I wanted to destroy a charge of conspiracy and thought this was the best way. It fitted my pattern of Not Getting Caught. Even though we fought, we were all together.

The first blood I saw in Chicago was the blood of Stu Albert, Jerry's closest friend. It happened in the first Sunday afternoon police riot in Lincoln Park. I embraced Stu, crying and swearing – sharing his blood. I went up to the cops and shook my fist. I made a haranguing speech, standing between rows of pig cops and scared spectators of the music festival, which of course by now was over. That kind of unity that Stu and I have, even though he is a Marxist-Leninist and I am a fuck-off, is impossible to explain. We are united in our determination to smash this system by using any means at our disposal and build a new world. In any event it didn't matter. Jerry's big Pig hit the Civic Center and Mrs. Pig was let loose in the park hours later, screaming that her thirty sons would avenge her husband's arrest. I dropped the hint that we were considering running a lion. In the end thousands of pigs were used, real pigs, pig buttons, nice pigs like Mr. and Mrs. Pig (see wonderful photo in Chicago *Daily News* entitled "Mr. & Mrs. Pig Re-United in the Pokey") and bad pigs like the cops, Daley, Humphrey and the politicians. It was shades of Animal Farm and you couldn't tell the pigs from the farmers or the farmers from the pigs. On the last day, I knew we had won when I saw Humphrey and Daley on TV and in photos. Everyone could see they were coming up Pig as all hell. As a familiar chant, one that I had never heard at any demonstration, put it – "The Whole World is Watching! The Whole World is Watching!" Thanks again to Mayor Daley for beating up Walter Cronkite.

Myths work the way this section was written. They just go. The next section will also be called "Getting It All Out There" to make some more non-points. Anyway, repetition is the key to advertising. "Drink Revolution and See."

GETTING IT ALL OUT THERE (again)

America is Racist.
America is Imperialistic.
Police are Brutal.
Mass media distort.
Bah — Bah — Bah — Bah — Bah — Bah — Bah — Bah — .Bah
Here we go again. None of these phrases contains information.
I never once accused the police of being brutal, for example.
That was not my role; there were enough liberals to do that.°
I applauded the police performance. They were major life-
actors, performed brilliantly and never let us get away without
a proper cop response. They were pigs through and through.
Those that weren't, played different roles. You didn't have to
worry about them, anyway. They weren't performing for the
whole world and besides they were only worried about keeping their jobs and not about killing you and your brothers.

I have a certain hesitancy about the term "pig" in reference
to police. Don't get me wrong, the term is perfect but not
enough of an insult if that's your message. Cops like to be
called pigs and Nazis and fascists and killers. It lends itself to

° As I write this, for example, I know damn well that I'll pick up the
New York *Times* Sunday edition tomorrow and find a full page ad in
the News of the Week in Review section, sponsored by some Ad Hoc
Concerned Citizens for a Calm Chicago attacking the police for their
brutality. Galbraith, MacDonald, Howe, maybe even Arthur Gold-
berg and John Lindsay (we cut pretty high on the hog in Chicago).
It will cost over $6,000 and is the liberals' way of burning money,
relieving their guilt and getting their name in the paper. As far as
I'm concerned, it's a waste. That's the nice thing about liberals,
though, even though you tell 'em to fuck off they'll still be around.
If you don't believe me, read tomorrow's *Times*.

the image of masculinity they try to preserve. When I get pissed at cops it goes something like this: "You fuckin' fag-ass cocksuckers! You commie pimps! You Jew-bastard fags! You get your fuckin' paws off me, you bunch of cowards! I can kick your fuckin' ass in! I'll bet you fuck each other up the ass. How come you guys never get laid?" That's cop talk. That spooks 'em. You can hurt their feelings. Establish rapport. Scare them or get your ass kicked some more. Psychic jiu-jitsu always has its risks but you always get the message through. I use it every day to stay alive.

*   *   *   *

SCENE

Packed jail cell generally called "the Tank" in cop talk. The last stop on my tour of Chicago jails; only a door and a thin corrugated metal wall separate us from the courtroom (the wall makes a hell-of-a-racket when you kick it).

ACTORS

Me.   One naked guy named Brother Michael (I renamed him Iron Mike), whom they caught running bare-ass through the Loop. Iron Mike sits in the Lotus Position in the corner and never speaks. Twenty to twenty-five pacifists, all professionals, dressed in calm, well-groomed Quaker-meeting-hall clothes. They all look like Staughton Lynd. They were arrested in a vigil near the Amphitheater. I knew it without even asking. One Fat Pig, who keeps opening the door to the courtroom calling a name and always correcting the pronunciation himself.

CONFLICT

I don't want to fuck up the pacifists' theater (Iron Mike and me already explained ourselves to each other and are brothers. A brother is someone who likes you so much he doesn't give a shit what you do.) Yet I still want to do my own play. I keep meeting them half-way, explaining what I'm doing. I'm talking with one of them, a guy who looks the model of a successful young doctor, calm, well-groomed. I'm explaining theater and getting it all out there, though my voice is hoarse from explaining and tear gas. Each time the door opens with Fat Pig on the doorknob, a shy kid says something like, "Please sir, can we have some water?" or "Please sir, can we make a call, it's been ten hours?"

"Hey kid, you ain't getting through. Don't you see that? It's just like your silly-assed vigil. You're begging an America that won't listen. Besides, it's not even good begging. You could use a lesson from the St. Marx Panhandlers. Iron Mike over there in the corner is saying more than you and he ain't saying nothing. Watch, I'll show you how to beg and then I'll do my thing without physical violence, 'cause I know you are pacifists. Hang on."

THE PLAY BEGINS

The door opens and there is Fat Pig. I dash across the cell, throw myself at his feet, clutching his pants. "Sir! Sir!" I plead, "We have no food! We have no water! Please, sir!" Fat Pig is really shook. He pushes me with his legs, not a real kick but a push. I jump up. "You motherfucker fag! Come on in here, I'll kick the shit out of you! You fat bastard! I got a black belt in karate" and I prove it by doing some fancy chops that I saw in some movie, yelling "Ya! Ya! Wash-hoi! Wash-hoi!" Fat Pig is totally astonished. He shouts, "You coward! You coward!" He must be confusing me with the pacifists. Anyway, I know I've got him when he sinks to my level of rationality. Coward? He's three times my size. But that doesn't matter, I can kick the shit out of him any time I want 'cause I ain't afraid to die and he's afraid of losing his job. I don't know if the pacifists got the point. I didn't even ask them. When you're an artist, your art is the point as well as the reason you keep going. Applause, boos, analysts, critics are all irrelevant. That's one reason I never respond to criticism and always suspect those that do, for example, Norman Mailer. Those that respond are politicians, they want everyone to love them. Artists never "need" love. I learned this from Saul Alinsky, radical street organizer, whom I consider a fantastically great artist. He told me once about three years ago, as we sat in a Boston hotel room drinking Scotch and discussing organizing, "Never respond to criticism or else you'll be doing everybody's thing but your own." I picked Alinsky's brain clean that night.

5

ON TO CHICAGO

FESTIVAL OF LIFE
August 25–30

CHICAGO

Produced by Marshall McLuhan

Directed by Mayor Daley and Antonin Artaud

The medium is the mess.

— MARSHALL McLu

The policeman isn't there to create disorder. He's there to preserve disorder.

— MAYOR RICHARD J. DALEY,
Press Conference, September 10, 1968

Theater of Cruelty proposes to resort to a mass spectacle; to seek in the agitation of tremendous masses, convulsed and hurled against each other, a little of that poetry of festivals and crowds when, all too rarely nowadays, the people pour out into the streets . . . The theater must give us everything that is in crime, love, war or madness if it wants to recover its necessity . . . We want to create a believable reality which gives the heart and senses that kind of concrete bite which all true sensation requires . . . We wish to address the entire organism through an intensive mobilization of objects, gestures and signs, used in a new spirit. The Theater of Cruelty has been created in order to restore a passionate and convulsive conception of life and it is in this sense of violent rigor and extreme condensation of scenic elements that the cruelty on which it is based must be understood. This cruelty, which will be bloody when necessary but not systematically so, can thus be identified with a kind of severe moral purity which is not afraid to pay life the price it must be paid.

— ANTONIN ARTAUD, *The Theater and Its Double*

THE YIPPIES
ARE GOING TO CHICAGO

Last December a group of us in New York conceived the Yippie! idea. We had four main objectives:

1. The blending of pot and politics into a potlitical grass leaves movement — a cross-fertilization of the hippie and New Left philosophies.

2. A connecting link that would tie together as much of the underground as was willing into some gigantic national get-together.

3. The development of a model for an alternative society.

4. The need to make some statement, especially in revolutionary action-theater terms, about LBJ, the Democratic Party, electoral politics, and the state of the nation.

To accomplish these tasks required the construction of a vast myth, for through the notion of myth large numbers of people could get turned on and, in that process of getting turned on, begin to participate in Yippie! and start to focus on Chicago. *Precision was sacrificed for a greater degree of suggestion.* People took off in all directions in the most sensational manner possible:

"We will burn Chicago to the ground!"

"We will fuck on the beaches!"

"We demand the Politics of Ecstasy!"

"Acid for all!"

"Abandon the Creeping Meatball!"

And, all the time: "Yippie! Chicago — August 25–30."

Reporters would play their preconceived roles: "What is the difference between a hippie and a Yippie?" A hundred different answers would fly out, forcing the reporter to make up his own answers; to distort. And distortion became the life-blood of the Yippies.

Yippie! was in the eye of the beholder.

Perhaps Marshall McLuhan can help.

This is taken from an interview in the current Columbia University yearbook:

MCLUHAN: "Myth is the mode of simultaneous awareness of a complex group of causes and effects . . . We hear sounds from everywhere, without ever having to focus . . . Where a visual space is an organized continuum of a uniform connected kind, the ear world is a world of simultaneous relationships. Electric circuitry confers a mythic dimension on our ordinary individual and group actions. Our technology forces us to live mythically, but we continue to think fragmentarily, and on single, separate planes."

INTERVIEWER: "What do you mean by myth?"

MCLUHAN: "Myth means putting on the audience, putting on one's environment. The Beatles do this. They are a group of people who suddenly were able to put on their audience and the English language with musical effects — putting on a whole vesture, a whole time, a *Zeit.*"

INTERVIEWER: "So it doesn't matter that the Pentagon didn't actually levitate?"

MCLUHAN: "Young people are looking for a formula for putting on the universe — *participation mystique.* They do not look for detached patterns — for ways of relating themselves to the world, a la nineteenth century."

So there you have it, or rather have it suggested, because myth can never have the precision of a well-oiled machine, which would allow it to be trapped and molded. It must have the action of participation and the magic of mystique. It must have a high element of risk, drama, excitement and bullshit.

Let's return to history. Remember a guy named Lyndon Johnson? He was so predictable when Yippie! began. And then *pow!* He really fucked us. He did the one thing no one had counted on. He dropped out. "My God," we exclaimed. "Lyndon is out-flanking us on our hippie side."

Then Go-Clean-for-Gene and Hollywood-Bobby. Well, Gene wasn't much. One could secretly cheer for him the way you cheer for the Mets. It's easy, knowing he can never win. But Bobby, there was the real threat. A direct challenge to our theater-in-the-streets, a challenge to the charisma of Yippie!

Remember Bobby's Christmas card: psychedelic blank space with a big question mark — "Santa in '68?" Remember Bobby on television stuttering at certain questions, leaving room for the audience to jump in and help him agonize, to battle the cold interviewer who knew all the questions and never made a mistake.

Come on, Bobby said, *join the mystery battle against the television machine.* Participation mystique. Theater-in-the-streets. He played it to the hilt. And what was worse, Bobby had the money and power to build the stage. We had to steal ours. It was no contest.

Yippie stock went down quicker than the money we had dumped on the Stock Exchange floor. Every night we would turn on the TV set and there was the young knight with long hair, holding out his hand (a gesture he learned from the Pope): "Give me your hand — it is a long road ahead."

When young longhairs told you how they'd heard that Bobby turned on, you knew Yippie! was *really* in trouble.

We took to drinking and praying for LBJ to strike back, but he kept melting. Then Hubert came along exclaiming the "Politics of Joy" and Yippie! passed into a state of catatonia which resulted in near permanent brain damage.

Yippie! grew irrelevant.

National action seemed meaningless.

Everybody began the tough task of developing new battlegrounds. Columbia, the Lower East Side, Free City in San Francisco. Local action became the focus and by the end of May we had decided to disband Yippie! and cancel the Chicago festival.

It took two full weeks of debate to arrive at a method of dropping-out which would not further demoralize the troops. The statement was all ready when up stepped Sirhan Sirhan, and in ten seconds he made it a whole new ball game.

We postponed calling off Chicago and tried to make some sense out of what the hell had just happened. It was not easy to think clearly. Yippie!, still in a state of critical shock because of LBJ's pullout, hovered close to death somewhere between the 50/50 state of Andy Warhol and the 0/0 state of Bobby Kennedy.

The United States political system was proving more insane than Yippie!.

Reality and unreality had in six months switched sides.

It was *America* that was on a trip; we were just standing still.

How could we pull our pants down? America was already naked.

What could we disrupt? America was falling apart at the seams.

Yet Chicago seemed more relevant than ever. Hubert had a lock on the convention: it was more closed than ever. Even the squares who vote in primaries had expressed a mandate for change. Hubert canned the "Politics of Joy" and instituted the "Politics of Hope" — some switch — but none of the slogans mattered. We were back to power politics, the politics of big-city machines and back-room deals.

The Democrats had finally got their thing together by hook or crook and there it was for all to see — fat, ugly, and full of shit. The calls began pouring into our office. They wanted to know only one thing: "When do we leave for Chicago?"

What we need now, however, is the direct opposite approach from the one we began with. We must sacrifice suggestion for a greater degree of precision. We need a reality in the face of the American political myth. We have to kill Yippie! and still bring huge numbers to Chicago.

If you have any Yippie! buttons, posters, stickers or sweatshirts, bring them to Chicago. We will end Yippie! in a huge orgasm of destruction atop a giant media altar. We will in Chicago begin the task of building Free America on the ashes of the old and from the inside out.

A Constitutional Convention is being planned. A convention of visionary mind-benders who will for five long days and nights address themselves to the task of formulating the goals and means of the New Society.

It will be a blend of technologists and poets, of artists and community organizers, of anyone who has a vision. We will try to develop a Community of Consciousness.

There will be a huge rock-folk festival for free. Contrary to rumor, no groups originally committed to Chicago have dropped out. In fact, additional ones have agreed to participate. In all about thirty groups and performers will be there.

Theater groups from all over the country are pledged to come. They are an integral part of the activities, and a large amount of funds raised from here on in will go for the transportation of street theater groups.

Workshops in a variety of subjects such as draft resistance, drugs, commune development, guerrilla theater and underground media will be set up. The workshops will be oriented around problem-solving while the Constitutional Convention works to developing the overall philosophical framework.

There will probably be a huge march across town to haunt the Democrats.

People coming to Chicago should begin preparations for five days of energy-exchange. Do not come prepared to sit and watch and be fed and cared for. It just won't happen that way. It is time to become a life-actor. The days of the audience died with the old America. If you don't have a thing to do, stay home, you'll only get in the way.

All of these plans are contingent on our getting a permit, and it is toward that goal that we have been working. A permit is a definite contradiction in philosophy since we do not recognize the authority of the old order, but tactically it is a necessity.

We are negotiating, with the Chicago city government, a six-day treaty. All of the Chicago newspapers as well as various pressure groups have urged the city of Chicago to grant the permit. They recognize full well the huge social problem they face if we are forced to use the streets of Chicago for our action.

They have tentatively offered us use of Soldiers' Field Stadium or Navy Pier (we would have to re-name either, of course) for our convention. We have had several meetings, principally with David Stahl, Deputy Mayor of Chicago, and there remains but to iron out the terms of the treaty — suspension of curfew laws, regulations pertaining to sleeping on the beach, etc. — for us to have a bona fide permit in our hands.

The possibility of violence will be greatly reduced. There is no guarantee that it will be entirely eliminated.

This is the United States, 1968, remember. If you are afraid of violence you shouldn't have crossed the border.

This matter of a permit is a cat-and-mouse game. The Chicago authorities do not wish to grant it too early, knowing this would increase the number of people that descend on the city. They can ill afford to wait too late, for that will inhibit planning on our part and create more chaos.

It is not our wish to take on superior armed troops who outnumber us on unfamiliar enemy territory. It is not their wish to have a Democrat nominated amidst a major bloodbath. The treaty will work for both sides.

There is a further complicating factor: the possibility of the Convention being moved out of Chicago. Presently there are two major strikes taking place by bus drivers and telephone and electrical repairmen, in addition to a taxi strike scheduled to begin on the eve of the Convention.

If the Convention is moved out of Chicago we will have to adjust our plans. The best we can say is, keep your powder dry and start preparing. A good idea is to begin raising money to outfit a used bus that you can buy for about $300, and use locally before and after Chicago.

Prepare a street theater skit or bring something to distribute, such as food, poems or music. Get sleeping bags and other camping equipment. We will sleep on the beaches. If you have any free money we can channel this into energy groups already committed. We are fantastically broke and in need of funds.

In Chicago contact *The Seed*, 837 N. LaSalle St.; in New York, the Youth International Party, 32 Union Sq. East. Chicago has rooming facilities for 25 organizers. Write us of your plans and watch the underground papers for the latest developments.

The point is, you can use Chicago as a means of pulling your local community together. It can serve to open up a dialogue between political radicals and those who might be considered hippies. The radical will say to the hippie: "Get together and fight, you are getting the shit kicked out of you." The hippie will say to the radical: "Your protest is so narrow, your rhetoric so boring, your ideological power plays so old-fashioned."

Each can help the other, and Chicago — like the Pentagon demonstration before it — might well offer the medium to put forth that message.

POSTSCRIPT

The preceding article, borrowed from *The Realist*, July 7, 1968, is the only article I wrote about Chicago prior to the Convention. It was quoted by Jack Mabley of the Chicago *American* as "proof" of my serious revolutionary goals. It was also quoted in a subsequent article in the Chicago *Sun-Times*, entitled "Cops Watch Top Yippies," an article which showed only that they watched what we wrote in the underground press. Both news articles quote the opening section of my piece, the part with the numbers (both, incidentally, changed the word "potlitical" back to "political"). STRUCTURE IS MORE IMPORTANT THAN CONTENT IN THE TRANSMISSION OF INFORMATION. It is the same as saying "the medium is the message." The fact that they quoted the section with the numbers reminds me of how I used to bull my way through college exams. If I didn't know the answer to a question such as "Why did the Tasmanian Empire collapse?" I made a point of structuring the answer in the following manner:

Economically, the Tasmanian Empire suffered from bureaucratic excesses and internal corruption. It became . . .

Culturally, a decline could be noted in the quality and character of artistic output. In previous times . . .

Politically, the Tasmanians, although they had developed one of the most advanced forms of government, found themselves with a system which steadily grew more unworkable. It was necessary . . .

The teacher always considered this "structure" worthy of serious consideration. I never studied in college, I just practiced outlines, played games, and got laid.

*   *   *   *

Victor Riesel, in a column titled "Yippie Riots Long Planned," writes about the article: "In a publication called *The Realist*, edition #82, **FREE**, Yippie leader, talks of burning down Chicago and arranging a massive orgy on the beaches. It is all there — the plans for the abortive march on the Amphitheater, the strategy for disturbing the delegates, the talk of raiding the hotels, bars and nightclubs." Maybe you can find that in the article. I'm having a tough time, but then of course I don't have the advantage of being blind.

A NON-RESPONSE
TO THE DOUBTING THOMASES

Abe's got an article somewhere in the *Seed*; I haven't read it, but I'll respond anyway. It says, "Don't come to Chicago," not outright, but between the lines. It says Chicago Free City Survival has pulled out of the Yippie! Festival and the heavies from New York are running the show. I hope he points out that Chicago Yippies also signed the permit request and all the local Yippies, even those who chickened out, are working on the Festival harder than ever. Maybe "chickened out" is too strong, maybe "realistic" is less of a down. I'm sure the city officials have reminded the local Yippies that they have to stay in Chicago while the rest of us can do our thing and fade into the night. Which is true and understandable. The only reason there was a permit mix-up was that Chicago people kept telling us that it was on its way. They were a bit naïve on this and other things, but they haven't experienced the Pentagon, Grand Central Station, large Be-ins and negotiations with city officials who take you for a ride. Secondly, the Chicago hip community, unlike the communities of other large urban cities, is small and spread out. That's probably why the *Seed* often sounds like it's put out by people writing to each other. It is not a Movement paper, but a family affair. That's not a put down. The *Seed* is a Movement paper that teaches by example — LOOK WE ARE A FAMILY — HERE IS OUR SOUL — WE DO OUR THING, YOU DO YOURS, it's an important message. But they are a flower family, and the plum blossoms have taken to the hills, they have left the city's cellars, beaten out by cops' billy clubs. The *Seed* is the last in the line of flower papers. Gone is the San Francisco *Oracle*, gone to the hills; gone is the

L.A. *Oracle*, off to the seashore; gone is the Boston *Avatar*, born anew by the valley people.

Tougher — that's it, TOUGHER. Not "political," as Abe would say. What the fuck does political mean? PO–LI–TI–CAL.

How can a newspaper such as the *Seed*, which is supposed to be in the Zen tradition, and which professes to understand correctly the idiocy of categories and separation, persist in labeling things political or apolitical? Is fighting for your right to be in the park political?

Tell me, *Seed*, what if doing your thing is "political," what if you consider doing your thing as your definition of politics? And what if your thing is what you call politics? We meditated at the Pentagon. How can you define joy — Festival of Joy? Joy–Toy–Joy–Boy–Joy. Joy is picking flowers in the woods. Joy is punching a cop when he steps on your toe. Joy is diving off the rocks at Hyde Park into smashing waves. Joy is saying no and living no to a government grown old and evil. Joy is doing what you want to do. Joy is living in history — change that, Joy is *doing* in history. Joy is none of these things in the end. Joy is just another name for an American liquid soap. Bubble! Bubble! If you want to have the most together, exciting, intense time of your life, you can have it in Chicago. Abe and the other *Seed* people wouldn't miss it, or they wouldn't be working so hard on it. If they want a Festival of Life, and they are working on it, why won't it happen? They got paranoia. Paranoia is when you look in the future, see gloom, then run and hide in the past. The future's in your head. Chicago is a big city, actions and activities are spread out. Those that act peacefully will be treated peacefully; in fact, they will be held up as models of the good niggers. There'll be everything happening here. All kinds of politics. People will visit the Zoo, people will sell newspapers, and others will debate your ideology and march on the Amphitheater and dance in the park and give out food, and swim, and smoke dope, and fuck, and fight cops and give cops flowers and get pregnant and laugh and cry and live and die and there will be a whole mess of people here doing the same and yet no one will be doing what you're doing. Festival of Life is what will happen, only real LIFE — not some *Time Magazine* fag version of Hippie Heaven. We are Yippies, not hippies. Chicago is your trip. Don't you want it that way?

THIS IS WHAT HAPPENED

The reader should write or draw in the space above HIS CHICAGO. More paper can be stolen at any stationery store. The rest is my trip. It is by no means everything that happened or that I learned. I could never get all that down on paper. Not in a million years I couldn't.

CREATING THE PERFECT MESS

Perhaps the best way to begin to relate to Chicago is to clear your throat of the tear-gas fumes, flex your muscles, stiff from cop punches, write lying down, collapsing from fifteen solid days on no more than three hours sleep each night, mouth OM, smile, and then roll on the floor laughing hysterically. I can only relate to Chicago as a personal anarchist, a revolutionary artist. If that sounds egotistical, tough shit. My concept of reality comes from what I see, touch, and feel. The rest, as far as I'm concerned, didn't happen. If it did, so what, then it happened. Great! I am my own leader. I make my own rules. The revolution is wherever my boots hit the ground. If the Left considers this adventurism, fuck 'em, they are a total bureaucratic bore. SDS came to Chicago to talk to the McCarthy kids. We came to have the McCarthy kids experience what we as long-hairs experience all the time—the experience of living in a police state and the beauty of our alternative society. Today I stand safe on the corner of St. Marx Place and the headline reads: POLICE INVADE McCARTHY HEADQUARTERS AND CLUB CAMPAIGN WORKERS. It is the final scene in the Theater of Cruelty played out in Chicago. Another week and we could have gotten the cops to assassinate Humphrey.

We had won the battle of Chicago. As I watched the acceptance speech of Hump-Free (new slogan: Dump the Hump and Vote for Free) I knew we had smashed the Democrats' chances and destroyed the two-party system in this country and perhaps with it electoral politics. Nixon–Agnew vs. Humphrey–Muskie. Four deuces. HA! HA! Losers ALL!* There was no doubt in my

* See McLuhan's brilliant article in a recent *Saturday Evening Post* entitled "All the Candidates Are Asleep."

mind when I saw that acceptance speech that we had won. There would be a Pig in the White House in '69. I went out for champagne, brought it up to the MOB office, and toasted the Revolution. Put on my dark glasses, tucked my hair under my hat, pasted on my mustache, and called my wife. Told her to ditch the Chicago police tailing us and pick me up. I checked my phony identification cards and my youth ticket. In a half hour we were at O'Hare Airport, two hours later back on the Lower East Side.

All the way on the plane I kept wondering what the fuck we would have done if they had let us stay in Lincoln Park at night. As usual the cops took care of the difficult decisions. The concept of the Pig as our leader was truer than reality. It was the perfect symbol. We love the Pig! (our candidate and leader). We hate the Pig! (Daley, cops, authority). Everything is Pig . . . Chicago is total garbage and the pigs ate like politicians. The pigs that attacked us in the park lived in the Zoo, housed in the Lincoln Cultural and Arts Center. One of the pigs that killed Dean Johnson, a seventeen-year-old Indian brother from Sioux City, our only martyr, in what was allegedly self-defense, was called Officer Manley.* The liberal schmuck deputy mayor who stalled for four months on our permit application was named David Stahl. The federal judge who was to hear our lawsuit was named Lynch (we whipped him by taking back the suit and remarking that we had as little faith in the judicial system of this country as we did in the political). The names and coincidences were beyond belief.

Symbols and myths is what it's all about. Headlines: NATIONAL GUARD VS. THE HIPPIES AT CONRAD HILTON. My God, the overground press looked like the *East Village Other*. It was impossible to tell who was who. A perfect and total mess. The cops drove us out in the street each night, teaching us how to survive and fight. How could city Yippies totally unorganized

---

* Mayor Daley's unbelievable 70-page whitewash of what happened in Chicago states, "No one was killed or seriously injured." There seem to be a number of realities floating around.

(although very together) take on superior armed forces in unfamiliar territory resembling the countryside? We had to leave but we never retreated! Let us make that point crystal clear. We dispersed. We persisted in fighting for our right to stay in the park the total time we were in Chicago. In fact we were really fighting for our right to be in Grant Park, which was our original intention (check our first articles as well as the original permit application filed on March 25th). For it was Grant Park, right across from the Headquarters of the Chief Pigs, the Conrad Hitler, largest hotel in the world, that was Circus Ring Number One.

Fifteen days ago I was left in Chicago by the other troublemakers who had things to put together in New York before heading back. I had a dollar in my pocket, which I ceremoniously burned in the *Seed* office, and said, "Now I am ready for the battle." I bummed a few bucks from Abe Peck, the editor, and was off and running. I bought a little red book in Woolworths which incidentally fell apart, revealing scraps of Chinese newspapers which I later showed to police to prove conclusively that the Yippies were linked directly to Red China. By the time I was through I had the home phone numbers of the Chief of Police, Deputy Mayor, Hubert Humphrey's credit card number (also the address where he was really staying – the Astor Tower Hotel – his office staff and aides stayed at the Hilton) and information on all the key people in Yippie!, MOB, press, police and resource people (those who had trucks, food, banners, pigs, buttons). I had a lot of information. Information is the key to survival. Information is what the struggle is all about. As long as I knew what I was doing better than the people I encountered knew what they were doing, I would survive. If not, I would die. I had no doubts about that. Knowing what to do was the way not to get caught. As I said to the cops who came to arrest me Wednesday as I was sitting in the Lincoln Hotel Restaurant waiting for breakfast, "The first duty of a revolutionist is to get away with it. The second duty is to eat breakfast. I ain't going." It was a bust written by a Hollywood

screenwriter. I had painted the word FUCK on my forehead as
part of my costume. I didn't feel like having my picture in the
mass media that day and that is the only way to do it and still
be able to do your thing. Especially if your thing is heavy. My
hat was drawn low over the word because I didn't feel like
pissing off the waitress (we had already played out a number
of theater pieces in that restaurant). Two cops came in and
said, "We have a tip you have something under your hat, will
you please remove it." (Information: a phony cop. A real cop
never says please. Information: he won't be rough on you.)

"I'm going to eat. Want to join us?"

They had a conference.

"You guys better call Commander Brash." (Information: cops
are afraid only of losing their jobs; always call for their superi-
or, it shakes the shit out of them. I had noticed they were from
the 18th Precinct.) They left. Soon they returned with six other
cops. Outside were four patrol cars. Out came their guns. "Take
off your hat." I lifted the gray ranger hat, one of the hundred
different disguises I had used that week, and shouted "BANG-
BANG." Krassner went hysterical, even my wife, who usually
worries, was smiling. The cops reached over and pulled me out
across the table, with me clutching a slice of bacon (oink!),
dragged me out of the restaurant, slammed me against a car,
handcuffed me, and took me in. I was kept incommunicado for
thirteen hours with no phone calls, no lawyers, no food (five
hours without water). I was transported from precinct house to
precinct house while fat dumb cops beat the shit out of me.
One cop, Officer Henley, showed me a gold bullet that he said
had my name on it. I fired back, "I have your name on a silver
bullet and I'm the Lone Ranger." Throughout the beatings I
kept laughing hysterically, "We whipped you fucking pigs, we
whipped your asses. You cocksuckers are afraid to lose your jobs
and we ain't afraid to die." The courtroom scene was a
shambles. I swore at the ACLU lawyer and told him to get his
liberal lawyers up here for a sit-in and forget about defending
me. In the hall I ripped up the arrest papers with all the

charges. It was all *Catch-22* bullshit anyway. I was really mad
though because they had succeeded in keeping me out of the
battle of Michigan Avenue. Actually I had worked out a perfect
plan not to get caught and still do my thing. At midnight the
night before, a girl with a brown cowboy hat covered with
blood was supposed to have run into the Lincoln Park area,
screaming that I had been killed. It would have worked too.
Lincoln Park at midnight just before the tear gas hit was the
best place in the country to begin that sort of spook story. It
was the hour of Paranoid's delight. (I remember hearing a kid
scream "the cops are coming" as he stared into a vacant field
with only trees. "Cops are blue, kid, and they come in large
numbers. Don't fire 'til you see the whites of their eyes.") Anyway, the girl didn't do it. Later she told me it was one of the
toughest decisions she ever made. She, more than most, realized
the power of myth. Anyway, the next day I really was flying.
It was the best. I rapped in Lincoln Park thanking Ho Chi
Minh for bringing the medical supplies, thanking Bob Dylan
for playing in the park, thanking Chairman Mao for the secret
plans ("Always have three plans — two from column A and one
from column B." Stage note: when the actor says Two he holds
up two fingers in the sign of the V, when he exclaims One he
jams one finger into the air, making the "up your ass" sign). I
thanked Marshall McLuhan for bringing his television set, I
thanked the Chicago cops and Mayor Daley, the founders of
the Yippies, for without their help none of this would have
been possible. I rapped about how leaders were full of shit, how
the MOB marshals were all cops, and how the politicians, Mc-
Carthy included, who came to the park to speak were fake
prophets. I told them the only way we could get to the amphitheater was to go as a community, to just ask the guy next to
you how to get there, if they didn't already know, and put your
arm around his shoulder and go with him. About five thousand
of us just headed for the Amphitheater down Michigan Avenue.
No leader, nothing. Just people. It was beautiful. Then the
chickenshit marshals took over. They are always the ones who

bring the megaphones and should never be trusted. In fact, if I ever see Eric Weinberger again I'm going to slice not only his megaphone but his throat as well. About ten blocks down Michigan Avenue the troops came out. It was unbelievable. Out comes the biggest fuckin' tank I ever saw. Me and this spade cat were in the middle of the block about then. (I had remembered Dana Beal's brilliant advice to a huge crowd: "When the shit hits the fan, the safest place is in the middle of the crowd.") I said to Frankie, my spade buddy, "Let's go up and fuck around." Eric was up there pissing in his pants, telling the people to sit down, which of course is the worst advice possible. I said, "Eric, put someone on the bullhorn who is not afraid to die, you are panicking people." I showed him. I went up and stretched out in front of the tank with one finger up in the air laughing like a son-of-a-bitch, while Frankie Spade slapped his thighs and roared.* Then I shouted out over the bullhorn, "You cops out there cool it, you hear! We just sent for the head cop and he'll be here in five minutes. You guys don't want to lose your jobs, do you?" Eric, even while I was speaking, would not give up the mike. Meanwhile Dick Gregory was having a most difficult time. He's a very funny guy but his politics are for shit and his street strategy is worse. I knew what was in his head all along. You know, front of the line, easy bust, suffer-jail-we-shall-over-come-fast-bullshit-masochistic theater — very manipulative. Because he only came out after the battle and also after he had tried his damnedest to scare people out of coming. I like him a lot but he's not ready for "any means necessary," at least not now on Michigan Avenue. I told him the rap to the cops was a bluff and my strategy was to get the head cop down here, grab him, and get us through. The other pigs (having a leader–follower head) wouldn't touch us. He said what if they did? I replied I would kill the Top Pig and I meant it. In three minutes, lo and behold a black limousine pulls up in the center of the

---

* A mistake. Better theater would have been to punch the tank or at least stand up roaring with laughter. I got co-opted by the pacifists.

crowd. I go up and say I want to see Chief Lynsky right away
or there will be more blood spilled here than in all the other
days together. A pig said, "I'm Lynsky's boss." I wasn't sure
but he sure had a lot of gold braid on. Pig Rocheford was his
name. He tried to get me to go with him in the car and discuss
this rationally. (Information: Top Pigs always act like liberals.)
"Oh no, I'm no leader. I'm just a wise-ass punk. We all have to
go or nobody goes." Meanwhile Eric hustles the Big Pig to the
mike, announcing, "We can go back to the park." The Chief Pig
and Eric are arm in arm, leading the sheep back to the meadow.
I'm going crazy but I think I can still win. I run back to the park
and hustle another bullhorn. Frankie Spade is the only guy I
can count on but he's passed out on the grass from the Super
Honey that came from our underground lab. So there we are on
the hilltop, Eric and the Chief Pig explaining very chummy how
we can all stay in the park and me announcing publicly the plan
to kidnap the Head Pig and snuff him if they touch us. I'm also
yelling for the Motherfuckers* because when the chips are
really down it's the Motherfuckers who would have the balls to
do it. (They had all vanished into the night, figuring it had all
been done.) Of course Gregory won out. He worked a deal with
the Chief, invited everyone up to his house, walking on the sidewalk. He got control of the bullhorns and monitors as fat as
cops had the people line up in threes; he put himself in front
with delegates from the Convention and marched the sheep
off to his house. I ran up and down the line laughing at the
sheep, telling them they were being taken for a ride, they'd
get in trouble following leaders, especially politicians. Even
Gregory's a politician. That's why he's running for President
and not voting for the Pig. I panhandled $80 in twenty minutes
from the sheep, telling them it was for Dope (even though it
would have been easier to tell them it was for Bail Money. I
bumped into one other cat named Tom who was working the

---

* The Up-Against-the-Wall Motherfuckers are a group of life-actor
anarchists who inhabit the cellars on the Lower East Side. They
enjoy scaring tourists and torturing pigs.

other side of the line with the Bail Bit — he made $150 and he's coming to the Lower East Side. I had finally found a brother.) Actually the money was to fly out of Chicago, 'cause it was over for me. I had seen that theater piece before: leaders with press buzzing around like flies get helped into the paddy wagons just before the sheep get slaughtered. As I walked away a kid said, "You afraid to join us?"

"You bet your ass I am. Besides, my leader is the Pig. I'll see you at the Inauguration."

"Are the Yippies going?"

"I doubt it."

There never were any Yippies and there never will be. It was a slogan YIPPIE! and that exclamation point was what it was all about. It was the biggest put-on of all time. If you believe Yippies existed, you are nothing but a sheep. The Brothers and Sisters who came and fought and made love weren't hustled. Everyone's Chicago came true. You know how I knew? Nobody was disappointed Bob Dylan didn't show up. You know he did, though it was just that the fuckin' Pigs wouldn't let him play in the park. I saw him. Sunday night we sat up in a tree near the Church of the Free Spirit in Lincoln Park smoking grass. If you don't believe me, go up to Woodstock and ask him.

September 1, 1968

THE N.Y. *TIMES* & ENTERING THE MYTH

The N.Y. *Times* is death on Yippie! I realized that last year when I participated in a press conference run by the Mobilization to announce plans for the Pentagon demonstration. There we were, a whole panel of people with me sitting on the end.

Each person did his rap in the style of his choice. My rap on the Exorcism was featured on all the television news shows. When the *Times* came out there was a picture of the panel. I was cut out of the picture. I went to school on that for a long time. Why was it so good for television and so rotten for the *Times?*

Chicago was, as I have stated before, a Perfect Mess. In a Perfect Mess everyone gets what he wants.* In a Perfect Mess only the System suffers. The road into Chicago begins and ends in your own head. Daley and the FBI will enter by finding a conspiracy. Jack Newfield will enter through his friend Tom Hayden. Richard Goldstein through me. Marvin Garson and the West Coast through Jerry Rubin. Paul Krassner will enter it through his own mind, as will Jerry Rubin, Allen Ginsberg, and Ed Sanders. Teen magazines will enter through interviews with young Yippie! girls (most of the interviews will be made up). Julius Lester will get it right. He always did.** The *Guardian* will enter it through SDS, as will *New Left Notes.* *Ramparts* will be mixed but its emphasis will be on politics rather than theater. The John Birch Society will enter it through Lester Maddox. The National Student Association will enter it through the McCarthy kids. Jean Genet's article for *Esquire* will be fascinating because Genet does not understand English. He will get it right. *Rolling Stone* will ignore it. *EVO* will enter it through the Lower East Side. Theodore White won't be able to enter it at all. *Meet the Press* will enter it through people like Allard Lowenstein, Muskie, McCarthy, and Dave Dellinger. Most interesting will be the way in which the Chicago *Seed* enters the Myth. The overground press in Chicago will white-wash what happened as soon as the blood is cleaned from the

---

* Even Daley, who, I think, wanted to show the world he was a tough Irish politician who wouldn't budge an inch once he had his mind set, got what he wanted.

** I highly recommend Julius' book, *Look Out Whitey! Black Power's Gon' Get Your Mama.*

streets. They have to live with Mayor Daley, not the Yippies. The *National Enquirer* will enter it through its own sexual fantasies.

Playboy will enter it through Hugh Hefner, who got beaten one night. Television news shows will enter it through Yippie! and the New York *Times* will enter it through the National Mobilization to End the War in Vietnam. There was enough of a Perfect Mess for everyone to get a share of the Garbage.

THE FESTIVAL BEGINS: SUNDAY, AUGUST 25, 1968

Jerry Rubin was the chief ideologist or scenario designer for the Festival of Life. My task was to design the symbols and gather up the props. We spoke recently about Chicago and again it was an argument about whose trip occurred. My position was that everyone's trip occurred. It was a do-your-own-thing theatrical mess. Jerry feels nothing happened in the park. I claim the park gave the movement its soul, its spiritual quality. I claim everything happened that is on the schedule I prepared,* with the possible exception of the beach party — because it was cold on the beach. The Yippie! Olympics might not have happened, but that was Krassner's idea, anyway. I have tons of garbage to prove my position and I am sure Jerry has tons to prove his. Our differences stem from our personalities and our attitude toward words. Maybe it's a debate between the red and the black. Jerry is much more serious. Ours might prove to be the greatest debate at this point in the Movement. Jerry wants to show the clenched fist. I want to show the

* See page 162 in "Some Props Used."

clenched fist and the smile. He wants the gun. I want the gun and the flower.

It's interesting, for example, that he thinks the music festival did *not* occur on Sunday as the schedule indicates. Incidentally the *Ramparts Daily Wall Poster* (which I thought fantastic, especially the first few editions) and the *Guardian* also stated that it did not occur. In truth, MC5 from Detroit played fantastic music for over an hour and Ginsberg followed with chanting and a guerrilla theater group did a mock rally with our own LBJ and Hump. At this point the fight over the truck ensued. I was for immediately bringing the truck, which was to serve as the stage, into the park despite police orders to the contrary. Ed Sanders was for sticking with what we had, namely, the band on the ground. My general approach was to try to use every prop that I had found. I hate waste. The guy who owned the truck was against bringing it in. I had to use a lawyer, a pretty girl, myself, and a lot of other tricks to convince him that not much could happen to the truck if the police confiscated it. He finally agreed. Ed Sanders had passed out from too much Honey. I rounded up Super Joel, who was dressed like a race-car driver with crash helmet and overalls. He had already been busted twice and was the guy who stuck the flower in a paratrooper's rifle at the Pentagon. He was perfect (as of course was everyone else in Chicago). I gave him the key to the truck and as it changed hands I knew he'd do it right. Peter Rabbit, a non-existent Yippie from the Lower East Side, climbed on the back with about seventy other Yippies. A whole crowd swarmed around fences and the truck. Police formed their first pig wall. I immediately called for the head cop. We were standing next to the front of the truck with Stu Albert. I explained the situation. "People in the back of the crowd can't see the musicians. The band has to be elevated. The people will all bunch up to the front and crush each other. It will be a very dangerous social problem" (a phrase I often use with city officials and head cops). "Well, Chief Lynsky will have to settle this," he replied. "He's got five minutes to get down here," I shot back. Stu loved it. Meanwhile the truck was allowed to go as close as it could get to the bandstand area, and two things occurred that were important. First, MC5 wanted to pack their equipment and leave because of the trouble they saw coming. Then, while I was working on that deal, I heard on my walkie-talkie that the cops were entering the park in the area south of the Free Zoo and the first battle of Lincoln Park had begun. The rest of the night was a series of forays by the cops into groups in the park. The official music festival was over. Police anarchy really broke loose.

For example, about 9 P.M. that night I was training a group of seven Yippies in developing gang strategy and unity (the Left calls these affinity groups, again showing their academic orientation) when I saw a crowd of people getting smashed near the fieldhouse. I went over to investigate, only to be clubbed and kicked by two cops. I returned to my original location and sent a runner to find Commander Brash, head of the 18th Precinct and currently on duty in the park. He came back telling me that Brash wanted to meet me at the Communication Center. I told him to go back and tell Brash to come over here. Two minutes later, Brash appeared. I said, "We have a legal right to be in the park until 11 P.M., isn't that correct?" "Yes," he replied. "Well, what the fuck are all these cops doing smashing us so soon? Can't you wait two hours? Where the hell's law and order in this town!" He agreed to pull the cops back until 11 P.M. Twenty minutes later a group of cops came charging around the fieldhouse and pushed and kicked us, ordering us out of the park. This was only one case of police anarchy. Either the cop in charge always broke his word or he never had control over his men; it made no difference — every agreement was broken. It made Chicago a moral as well as strategic victory for us. I considered it much better strategy to have the cops drive us out of the park each night. SDS and other groups which support Confrontation Politics rather than Being Politics tried to get people out in the streets sooner. Patience was at times a virtue.

Anyway, my strategy was to fight for every inch. That was the only way you could find out what was possible in Chicago. We had a two-hour fight, which we won, over plugging the electrical cable into the refreshment stand and finally there was MUSIC. Each little battle was exciting. The electric-cable fight was a big victory. Only the day before Chief Lynsky himself in the Pig Station (Lincoln Art and Culture Center) had sworn there would be no music in the park. He also swore that he would arrest me if I did anything wrong. He challenged me to kick him in the shins and I replied, "Only in front of NBC." I also gave a pep talk to the cops in the headquarters, saying "Don't let the National Guard steal your thunder." As I walked out of the building with my two cop tails I told them that all high level cops were phony liberals and full of shit. What I didn't tell them was two pieces of information that I picked up on this trip: 1) The cops were in a total state of disarray; walkie-talkies didn't work, they all had trouble with their different signals. I knew we would have better communication than they even if all our walkie-talkies were busted. 2) When I entered the police station, I noticed it was directly opposite 2100 North Lincoln Avenue. Up till then that building had been an ace in the hole. It had an interesting history. Four years ago the millionaire who had just renovated it went bankrupt. The apartment building was tied up in a court fight. It was totally empty and I had examined it through a cellar entrance five nights before in a very straight disguise. There was no electricity, the elevators didn't work, but it was totally habitable. It had one chain lock on the front door, which could be cut in 10 seconds. It could hold, counting the halls and everything, about 50,000 people, I estimated. There were two possible scenarios: 1) Grab it if it rained, which of course it never did. 2) Grab it on the last day and turn it over to the poor people of Chicago, making a statement about FREE RENT. However, I saw now that the location of the Police Headquarters rendered the building useless and I never thought about it again.

I guess we were discussing whether or not Jerry's trip or

my trip happened. Jerry's original article spelled YIPPEE! thus. The button I designed spelled it YIPPIE! Let the people decide. It sure will be a hell of a debate. Jerry's a tough-son-of-a-bitch. He's got a hell of a fuckin' ego. Almost as big as mine but not quite. The debate will go on in print only, for Jerry is a writer. I know I can whip him publicly because I'll use any means necessary. I also know he reads his speeches. It's knowing shit like that which makes me such a cocky punk. Also knowing that I have a flower in my fist helps.

HUSTLING & MYTH MAKING

Scene: Press conference held by MOB on Tuesday morning. I burst in with karate jacket, helmet, and heavy club made from the branch of a tree. I announce to the press that we are arming the Yippies and whatever the pigs dish into the park, we'll dish out. I keep slamming the club against my other palm.

REPORTER: Are you armed?
ME: I'm always armed.
REPORTER: Is that your weapon?
ME: This (holding club in the air and smiling), this is part of a tree. It symbolizes my love for nature.

The week before Chicago happened I did a sidewalk press conference as Frankie Abbott (the N.Y. *Times* said "Mr. Frank Abbott," naturally) and rapped about our schedule. Very gay until Wednesday night. Then I dropped the bomb: "We have an action planned for Wednesday night. We will announce it at a later date." ("Action" has a ring of trouble to it. You know, right eye closes, the word is spat out.) The next day Jack Mabley of the Chicago *American*, who wrote brilliantly about us, headlined his column "Yippie Leader a Put-On But Underneath Dead Serious." Some of the proof he used is interesting and I've discussed it in the Postscript to the article in *The Realist*.

Another way I enjoyed heightening the tension was in a response to an often asked question:

REPORTER: How many Yippies are in Chicago?
ME: Four (holding up four fingers). But we are bringing in four more on Wednesday (zap! up go the other four fingers).

This method of manipulating the media by using suspense to heighten the tension is extremely effective.

Some say I'm only in this for the publicity, which I have said jokingly too at times. I'll drop a clue, though, to fuck up their minds a little. Jack Laurence of CBS TV wanted to do an hour special on a day in my life, which I rejected as impossible unless I was also producer and director and could say "fuck." The point is, that's a big commitment and a pain in the ass. Besides, a day in my life is not with cameras and lights buzzing around. I know the hour is out there hanging, though, ready to be hustled for more. I constantly hustle the media. I make them pay as much as possible. Four cases of beer, limousine service, free dinner, press credentials. Once Channel 2 in Boston (where I socked in the only "horseshit" ever heard on Boston television) gave me a blank airplane ticket to fly back to New York. I filled in "Chicago" and got off at New York. I gave the ticket to Ellen, who was running Liberty House, to cash in on the difference. I suggested to *Life* Magazine that they could get some great photos if they threw 10,000 flowers out of a helicopter into Lincoln Park. They loved the idea. Then the bomb, "We'll only let you do it if you take one of our Newsreel° people up with you." They agreed. The flowers never showed though, but I think it was because the Newsreel team I gave

---

° The Newsreel is a New York-based operation designed to cover events as we see them happen. It is an integral part of our alternative society.

the information and contact to didn't follow it up. The *Life* guy was a good guy. Very young and sensitive. One of us, really. He let me live off his expense account. I refused two interviews with CBS because they wouldn't give me $500 I needed for 10,000 hot dogs I had located (a good price) with some help from Abe Feinglass, Vice President of the United Meat Packers Union. I had met him through an old college friend when I was hustling for Liberty House in Mississippi. His son, Bobbie, who also worked in Mississippi, and I were close friends. Abe and I talked about him at length. The truth of it is I never met Bob Feinglass, but what the hell, we probably would have been friends anyway.

Contrary to rumors I do not collect my press clippings. However, I'll save the one I saw yesterday in the New York *Post*. Here is a part of it:

YIP was born Oct. 21, 1967, with the march on the Pentagon, the event being heralded by a press release by **FREE**, whose personal fame has grown with the movement.

FREE ("I reject communism, socialism and/or capitalism") says he advocates LSD as a cure-all. Last year the 29-year-old radical led a hippie raid on the New York Stock Exchange, and wed his bride in a hippie ceremony in Central Park. In earlier years, he marched on Washington and Selma, Ala., was an East Coast leader of the Student Nonviolent Coordinating Committee, and has been arrested several times for civil rights and anti-war action.

At the last moment before the Democratic convention opened, when word had come of Mayor Daley's "defense" setup, **FREE** pleaded with the Yippies to stay home. Whether most of the 100,000 (including members of other protest groups such as the National Mobilization Committee to End the War) stayed home out of fear or whether a contingent that large ever really existed is debatable.

Other Yippie leaders include:

Jerry Clyde Rubin, 29, of Berkeley, Calif., a student at the University of California in the Mario Savio era, and active in the Free Speech Movement. In 1965 he became a staff member of the National Coordinating Committee Against the War in Vietnam. Dressed as a Revolutionary War soldier, he attended and was arrested at a meeting of the House Un-American Activities Committee in 1966.

Ed Sanders, 29, father of a daughter, and a poet, pacifist, vegetarian leader of the folk rock group called the Fugs and editor of a magazine with an unprintable name. He came to New York from Kansas City in 1957, enrolled at NYU, dropped out, and opened the Peace Eye Book Store at Tompkins Square in the East Village; in 1962 he was arrested for taking part in a sit-in at the Atomic Energy Commission to protest the dangers of nuclear testing.

They are "Leaders," but in quotation marks, because it is debatable whether the Yippies are (or ever were) a movement. In Grant Park Thursday afternoon Paul Krassner, editor of the *Realist,* declared the Yippies dead. But those were the names people identified when asked in Grant Park who the head Yippies were.

While troops listened over the loudspeaker, Krassner said: "Yippie was merely a slogan to bring together the New Left and the psychedelic dropouts . . . the Yippie never really existed," he added as he burned a poster with Mayor Daley's picture on it. "The pig on this poster is the King Yippie."

August 31, 1968

They have everyone fairly accurate but me. To begin with, I never issued a press release about the Pentagon. It was a TV shot which I go into in discussing the New York *Times* later on. I possibly said the quote. I never advocated LSD as a cure-all. I am not 29 years old. I never marched on Washington (if they mean the civil rights march of 1963, which I thought a phony and opposed) and never marched in the Selma march, although I've been in Selma four times and did help to coordinate clergymen in New England to make the trip. What the hell is an East Coast Leader of SNCC? I was active in New England Friends of SNCC but hardly an East Coast Leader. As far as me pleading with the Yippies to all stay home . . . no comment. That's a good prop to bring into court. The duty of a revolutionist is to stay out of jail.

I realize the media has tremendous power. I've had people come to my apartment yelling at me for saying certain things, clutching the news clipping in their hand. These are generally the same people who say they don't believe anything they read in the press. Hmm. Something fishy going on there . . . Why don't you have a whack at figuring it out? I already have.

Tuesday morning is chilly. I hustle my cop tails into driving me to North Beach. I walk across the sands and kneel next to Ginsberg and pick up the Indian chant "Hare-Hare, Hare-Hare, Krishna." I'm in my karate jacket and my club and helmet are at my side. I feel like the Samurai warrior in Church. The group is small and shivering under ragged blankets. I watch the gray waves of Lake Michigan roll against the beach. I notice the four patrol cars stationed on the roadway nearby. I cry real tears for about 10 minutes. I make a short speech about how this wasn't News in America. About how this wouldn't be on television that night but instead it would be shots of violence in the streets. I was very sad about that and cursed this fuckin' country. When I left, my tails said, "That's really strange, how can you go to that?" "A good politician always goes to church in the morning," I replied.

FIGURE & GROUND

The drawing on the next page is one of the most famous drawings in pyschology. What do you see when you look at it? Look again.

You probably have it by now. First you see a vase, then you see two faces. You cannot stare at the drawing for any length of time without experiencing the perceptual shift. The image that pops out, that appears to come between you and the page is the "figure," the background is called the "ground." When you see the faces you don't see the vase and vice versa. Try it.

Look at the next picture carefully. There is something hidden in it. There is a hidden figure . . . If you haven't found it by now search the upper right hand corner . . . There it is! A dog. Once you see it the dog becomes the figure and the remaining painting the ground. Once you know the dog is there you can never forget it. You can never look at this painting or even remember it without the dog coming to mind immediately.

Salvador Dali, "Apparition of Face and Fruit Dish on a Beach." *Courtesy Wadsworth Atheneum, Hartford*

I raise this point because I want to enter an important discussion about television coverage of demonstrations. I want to use figure and ground principles translated into information and rhetoric. We are the information on television, the rest is part of the rhetorical ground. We need about as much space to make our point as the dog in Dali's painting needs to make his.

We are not the only information on television. Advertisements, especially the best ones, have a fantastic amount of information. Watch, for example, *Meet the Press, Issues and Answers, Face the Nation,* or any of those boring, intellectual church-visitations on Sunday morning. Here is a typical one: a debate between a liberal and a conservative (not Vidal and Buckley — they are much more than rhetoric). The dry debate lasts about fifty minutes of the sixty allotted to the show. The other ten minutes are devoted to previews of the shows, station identification, and most importantly, commercials. Notice the way this ten minutes is treated as compared to the other fifty minutes. Notice the camera angles, cuts, flashes, zooms. Notice the play to the viewers' needs. Notice the appeal to "do what you've always wanted." The commercial is information. The program is rhetoric. The commercial is the figure. The program is the ground. What happens at the end of the program? Do you think any one of the millions of people watching the show switched from being a liberal to a conservative or vice versa? I doubt it. One thing is certain, though . . . a lot of people are going to buy that fuckin' soap or whatever else they were pushing in the commercial.

What would happen if a whole hour were filled with a soap commercial? That's a very interesting question and I will speculate that it would not work as well, which means that not as much information would be conveyed, that not much soap would be sold. It's only when you establish a figure–ground relationship that you can convey information. It is the only perceptual dynamic that involves the spectator.

Our actions in Chicago established a brilliant figure–ground relationship. The rhetoric of the Convention was allotted the fifty minutes of the hour, we were given the ten or less usually reserved for the commercials. *We were an advertisement for revolution.* We were a high degree of involvement played out against the dull field of establishment rhetoric. Watching the Convention play out its boring drama, one could not help but be conscious of the revolution being played out in the streets.

That underlying tension builds up and the viewer becomes totally involved with what we are doing EVEN IF HE CAN-NOT SEE OR EXPERIENCE IT DIRECTLY. He makes up what's going on in the streets. He creates the Yippies, cops, and other participants in his own image. He constructs his own play. He fabricates his own myth. Even if the media had decided on a total blackout of our activities, our message would have gotten through and perhaps with even more power. All people had to know was that America's children were getting slaughtered in the streets of Chicago and the networks were refusing to show it. WE CAN NEVER BE SHUT OUT. Not only would the public rebel against that form of censorship but also against the attempt to impose a dull ground upon an exciting figure. I'm sure what pissed off a good number of viewers was the fact that they were being forced to watch a dull, *Meet-the-Press,* Democratic Convention when, in fact, what they wanted to see was the Cops vs. Yippies football game taking place on the streets of Chicago.

KEY TO THE PUZZLE

THE KEY TO ORGANIZING AN ALTERNATIVE SOCIETY IS TO ORGANIZE PEOPLE AROUND WHAT THEY CAN DO AND MORE IMPORTANTLY WHAT THEY WANT TO DO.

It is this principle that differentiates Yippie! from IBM and from the Mobilization as well. There is no ideology except that which each individual brings with him. The role he plays in building the alternative society will shape in some way its ideology. If he plays a role of total involvement, he will develop a feeling that he created the myth in his own image. He will also recognize that others have created it in their image and that in reality the myth becomes a Gestalt. The myth is greater than the sum of its parts. Energy-centers that originate or gravitate to the center of the myth have to trust not only the myth, but also the vast numbers of participants who want to add their garbage to the pile. If it is bad garbage it will quickly rot, if it is good garbage it will help transform the pile into a shrine of holiness.

▲ **FREE** is the one with the mustache. The others are his friends from the Group Image/*Abramowitz,*© *Group Image Enterprises, 1968*

◀ **FREE** ready for battle in Newark. Ride 'em, **FREE**/*Ann Douglass*

There's **FREE** with her arm around her best friend. They are about to storm the Pentagon/*Judy Weiss* ▼

FREE is in the street again — this time celebrating the end of the war/*Ann Douglass*

FREE's the one carrying the cat with the flag/*Ann Douglass* ▼

▲ There's **FREE** helping kids get their thing together/*Roz Payne*

There's **FREE** rapping to friends in Lincoln Park/*Roz Payne* ▼

▲ **FREE**'s in the striped sweater. Smashed on Honey. He's off to the International Amphitheater with the other commies/*Ann Douglass*

◄ There's no room for **FREE** on the horse. She'll find another soon/*Ann Douglass*

There's **FREE** clownin' in the woods, stoned of course ▶

Robert Parent

6

FREE IS THE REVOLUTION

YIPPIE! IS FREE!

Free is the essence of Yippie! We operated Yippie! on less than $4,000 that we raised at a benefit and that we burned in a month. By the end of March we had no money, never used our bank account, had no meetings, had an office with no lock on the door and typewriters that would be liberated hours after they were donated. The non-leaders rarely visited the office, people who dropped in found themselves in a vacuum. They were forced to become leaders and spokesmen. They would answer the phones, distribute the leaflets, posters, stickers, and buttons. Everyone would answer the mail and Mitch Yippie would pick up the envelopes and sneak them through the postage meter at the place where he worked (he got caught and fired). The best article I read on Yippie! was written in a sex magazine called *Jaquar* and titled "an interview with the Queen of the Yippies." Most of us think it was totally fictitious, which, of course, makes it accurate. In Chicago we never really had an office although we used the *Seed*, Chicago's underground newspaper, as a coordination point (I was able to chisel two extra phones out of the phone company for the *Seed*, which was something McCarthy couldn't even do because of the telephone strike), and the Free Theater on North Lincoln Street as another center. After Sunday night, the Free Theater was turned into the Communication Center, hospital, sleeping area, music theater, and FREE STORE on a twenty-four-hour basis. Paul Sills, its director, told me how the whole experience has changed his ideas. If I ever go back to Chicago it will only be to see what's going on at the Free Theater.

The concept of FREE is one of the chief differences we had

with the MOB. Tuesday night we had a benefit at the Coliseum. We were to split the profits but we gave our share to the MOB — we would have burned it anyway. If I met people with money I would just ask them to come out to the park and dig what was happening. Some gave money, which we immediately "burned."

Thursday morning I visited the MOB office and found 20,000 copies of the *Rat* newspaper still wrapped up in one of the rooms. I asked this guy Lee what the fuck they were still doing there. "We want to sell them," he replied.

"To who? The whole thing's almost over. Why don't you just give them away?"

"How do you give them away?" he queried.

Slapping my forehead, I exclaimed, "Just throw them out the window!"

Late that night, just before I left Chicago, I stopped at the MOB office with the champagne. The newspapers were still there and for all I know still are.

THE FREE STORE

The FREE STORE lies at the center of our revolutionary vision. It is the key to organizing longhairs on the Lower East Side. Today there are hundreds who will fight to defend it, tomorrow there will be thousands. It breaks all the rules because it has only one: "THOU SHALT NOT STEAL FROM THE FREE STORE."

Everything is given away free at the FREE STORE and so it is inundated with garbage. When you open a FREE STORE America cleans out her cellar and dumps it in front of your door. America calls this charity and a FREE STORE is not about charity. A FREE STORE accepts no garbage. Return all garbage to its original owner with a map to the nearest garbage dump. Old clothes and books are garbage. Accept old clothes only if you have facilities (sewing machines or tie-dye operations) to turn the garbage into art. A FREE STORE dispenses ART, it does not dispense politics and it does not dispense garbage. For that you can always shop next door.

Everyone asks, "Who runs the FREE STORE?" There can only be one answer: "What do you want?" If you can help the customer then respond, "I run the FREE STORE." If you cannot help the customer then respond, "You run the FREE STORE."

There should be art on the windows and walls. The front should be particularly beautiful, to attract new customers. Making the store beautiful is the first order of business, keeping it beautiful is the second. The store can be called HEAVEN. HEAVEN is where you get whatever you want. You don't spit on the floor in HEAVEN. Paint stars on the ceiling, suspend fluffy clouds from the walls. Construct planets in the aisles. There should always be a supply of sandles, robes, wings and harps for those who wish to play clerk. Use Mylar on the walls. When you look at Mylar walls you look into your soul and smile. Cover the front with phosphorescent paint. It absorbs light and will glow at night. When people ask how the store is run, tell them "by the rays of the sun." In a FREE STORE there are no problems, there are only things to do. It is a free forum of theater in which the forces of art battle the forces of garbage. Who wins in unimportant, for the FREE STORE is a school and the student is repeatedly forced by the vacuum to choose sides. Which side are you on? Are you a garbage collector or are you an artist? The choice is always yours in a FREE STORE.

*   *   *   *

The FREE STORE is expanding in a variety of ways. We are currently redesigning the Astor Place Subway Station, constructing a park, and establishing a number of rent-free communes. In addition, Craft Training Programs (the Liberty House concept) are being set up in the building next door. In time we plan to liberate the whole Lower East Side and turn it into a FREE CITY. It will be the living model of the future. If the FREE STORE fails, we will carry the vision in our heads and try it again. We will never try what has succeeded in the past for in point of fact nothing has.

7

FREE ADVICE TO THE BROTHERS

MESSAGES TO THE BROTHERS
(to be accepted or rejected)

MAINTAIN A SENSE OF HUMOR. People who take themselves too seriously are power-crazy. If they win it will be hair-
cuts for all. BEWARE OF POWER FREAKS.

*   *   *   *

ALWAYS USE THE SYMBOLS, PROPS, DRESS AND LAN-
GUAGE OF THE PEOPLE YOU ARE WORKING WITH.
Never impose your language on people you wish to reach. If
you are working on the street do not talk of imperialism, participatory democracy, or affinity groups. Save that for college
seminars. Talk to the guys about getting fucked by the boss,
having a say in things, getting laid, and gangs. How would you
like to be known as the kid who got kicked out of your affinity
group?

*   *   *   *

IN A REVOLUTION, AS IN POOL HUSTLING, ONE
SHOULD USE ONLY AS MUCH FORCE AS IS NECES-
SARY TO PROVE ONE'S POINT, NO MORE, NO LESS.
The reason the U.S. Government will lose in Vietnam and that
Daley lost in Chicago is because they overact. As the militarists
would put it, they adopt a policy of overkill. When that hap-
pens they begin to devour themselves. Incidents such as police
clubbing Hugh Hefner are not unlike B52's bombing American
Marines with napalm. Neither the NLF nor the Yippies work
that way, we never eat our own.

*   *   *   *

WE CAN ONLY HAVE A REVOLUTION BASED ON
TRUST. One day in Chicago I got a message from a group in
Minneapolis that one of my closest friends was an FBI agent.
They furnished me with background material and an alias he

was supposed to have used there and in Milwaukee. That night I saw him and called him by his alias. "Hey Scott," I said. He didn't respond. I went up to him and handed him the note I had received. "Burn it," I said. He gave me some LSD that night and it was outasight. It could have been poison, I guess. No brother will ever give you poison, even by accident. Continually search for and surround yourself with brothers, it is your best means of survival.

*   *   *   *

THE FIRST DUTY OF A REVOLUTIONIST IS NOT TO GET CAUGHT. I discovered how to survive in the midst of chaos in Chicago. Use disguises, use different names, when you want to take care of business ditch your followers, bodyguards, reporters and establish good alibis. Reject all references to yourself as a leader. If you have to exert leadership let it be natural, arising out of the situation rather than your past history. The enemy always goes after the leaders. You should adopt the attitude that survival is the principal goal of the vanguard. You should avoid going to jail at all costs. If you are caught and put in jail, it is your revolutionary duty to escape. Going to jail presents people with the model of masochistic theater. Getting killed is the risk involved in living a revolutionary life to the fullest. I prefer death to prison. .

*   *   *   *

THE FIRST LINE OF DEFENSE IS. TO TURN ON THE ENEMY. Middle-of-the-roaders, cops, mothers, everybody should be hustled into the revolution. Under the uniform (the opposite of our costumes) of a cop exists a naked human being. Cops don't like to work, and have sex hang-ups just like everybody else. Ask one why he bothers working for a wife and kids that don't respect him. Ask him if he's getting laid enough. Take a lesson from Tokyo Rose, she was a damn good poolhustler. When you are trying to turn people onto the FREE society the first question you ask, even if you don't verbalize it, is: "What do you want?" What if the person answers "I want to kick the shit out of kids like you"? Build him a boxing ring.

NEVER EXPLAIN WHAT YOU ARE DOING. This wastes a good deal of time and rarely gets through. Show them through your action, if they don't understand it, fuck 'em, maybe you'll hook them with the next action.

*   *   *   *

RUN, DON'T WALK, TO THE NEAREST REVOLUTION. Wear out your shoes, get used to being exhausted. Eat only what you need and stay healthy if possible.

*   *   *   *

WHEN YOU MEET A BROTHER, NEVER PREACH TO HIM. Only exchange information such as date, time, place, and so on. Always respect the style of a brother. If he is doing your thing, you should not even waste time talking to him. Never preach to the already committed.

*   *   *   *

ALWAYS CREATE ART AND DESTROY PROPERTY. Become a work of art. Art is the only thing worth dying for.

*   *   *   *

NEVER FORGET THAT OURS IS THE BATTLE AGAINST A MACHINE NOT AGAINST PEOPLE. If, however, people behave like machines, treat them as such. If a machine slips on a banana peel we all laugh. If a person slips on a banana peel we help him off the ground. Our job is to line the streets of the country with banana peels.

*   *   *   *

REMEMBER THAT THE PEOPLE YOU ARE TRYING TO REACH OFTEN KNOW MORE THAN YOU. Learn from them. Last winter I spoke at a high school in Port Washington, New York. Two kids from junior high school, age fourteen and fifteen snuck into the room to listen to the rap. At the end the kids came up and told me I didn't know much. I asked them what they were into. "We sleep outside each night preparing ourselves for guerrilla fighting in the suburbs," they responded. One of the kids had been arrested four times in demonstrations and was about to be suspended for refusing to get a haircut. I went to school that day in Port Washington.

ADVICE TO MY BLACK BROTHERS:

PLANS FOR THE DESTRUCTION
OF THE UNIVERSITIES

Last fall I spoke at Cornell and announced, "The food here is free!" and twenty of us walked into the cafeteria, loaded our trays with hamburgers, Cokes, and pies and walked out without paying. We sat in the dining hall laughing and slapping each other on the back stuffing our faces with Digger shit. I told them of epoxy glue and what a great invention it was. And at another school we asked them why they were there and they said just to get a diploma and so we passed out mimeographed sheets that said "This is a diploma," and asked the question again.

We appeared at Brooklyn College and announced, "The classroom environment is free," unscrewed desk tops and transformed them into guns, passed out incense and art, wrote Black Board on the door, switched off the lights and continued in darkness, announcing that the security guard was one of us, freeing him through the destruction of his identity, and in general doing whatever spontaneously came to mind. Our message is always: Do what you want. Take chances. Extend your boundaries. Break the rules. Protest is anything you can get away with. Don't get paranoid. Don't be uptight. We are a gang of theatrical cheerleaders, yelling Go! Go! Go! We serve as symbols of liberation. That does not mean that at times we do not get caught. Everyone's been arrested or stomped on or censored or shot at or fired from a job or kicked out of school or all that and more. "We've all been snuffed," as Ed Sanders says. It is not the snuffing but the notion that we can get away with taking chances that keeps us going. The reason I believe world revolution is inevitable is because the National Liberation Front is

doing so well, not because they are getting slaughtered. Ché
Guevara went to Bolivia because they got away with it in Cuba.
The Movement grows through successes, not through frustra-
tion. The ability to withstand frustration is what keeps us alive.

Our brothers and sisters are in the prisons of the universities.
It is our duty to rescue them. Free men draw a line in Harvard
Yard and dare President Pusey to "cross over the line." Students burst into the dean's office and when he asks them what
they want they all hold a finger in the air. At San Francisco
State, Black Panthers and even White Panthers wait on the
rooftop ready to shoot if the administration calls the police onto
campus. Make war on bells in school. Bring alarm clocks to
class and have them ring on the half hour instead.of the hour.
You can buy a small Japanese tape recorder and a few speakers
from a junkyard for about twenty-five dollars. Some careful
camouflaging and you can suddenly turn the school into a huge
discothèque.

Columbia was a truly liberating experience for many of us.
Five buildings and five days forced people beyond the mere academic exercise of building a radical movement and into the more
relevant experience of building a radical community. White radicals must begin the development of radical communities near
universities and supported by sympathetic students. The experience of being in a radical movement lasts until the degree is
handed over. The experience of living in and constructing a radical community is of a much more durable quality.

8

SOME PROPS USED

This section contains some of the visual props I hustled for Chicago. "Hustled" means I designed them, stole the money to get them made, wrote them, transported and distributed them. It is just a sampling of the stuff I hustled. This doesn't mean that other people didn't help or that other people didn't hustle a whole lot of garbage for Chicago. They did. A week before it all happened we sat in Deputy Mayor Stahl's office at City Hall. I remarked that if all of us so-called ringleaders sat there for the next two weeks the Battle of Chicago would all happen anyway and probably happen better.

The leaflet entitled "Cops Eat Pie" was written and distributed by me on Mother's Day after the first Be-In in Lincoln Park. It was designed to help toughen a hippie-oriented Chicago community. We planned a music Be-In every Sunday until the Festival of Life in order to get the people of Chicago used to us. Needless to say, the cops did not heed the advice and sure enough, on August 25th we took to the streets.

The map of Lincoln Park appeared in most newspapers that I saw. It was better than a written story. It was a living advertisement for what we were doing. Look at it. Don't you want to hunt for the gold buried in Lincoln Park? Some say the map wasn't accurate. They are the cynics of our time. On Sunday beautiful white and green signs appeared throughout the Park, labeling each area. The FREE STORE gave out posters, buttons, dope, clothes, leaflets, and hundreds of other things. The stage was moved to the other end of the Music Area. The Communication Center was set up with tables, the central walkie-talkie, and a radio to monitor police calls. I know couples that got married in the Church of the Free Spirit. The Hospital was manned and in operation. When the Pigs came in at 11 P.M. that night they wrecked the reality of our vision. From then on we carried it in our heads, which is where we carried it all the time anyway.

The heading on the schedule, "TOP SECRET YIPPIE PLANS," was an idea I stole from an article in the Chicago Tribune titled "Secret Plans to Defend Convention Revealed."

The events on the schedule, as I have pointed out before, all happened, especially if you believe there can be such a thing as a "Workshop in Police Stupidity." I gave numerous workshops on such things as Gang Strategy, Guerrilla Theater as an Offensive and Defensive Weapon, and on Fucking the System. In the last I gave out the phone numbers of top city officials and police secret numbers. Each night I would spend time calling one pig, impersonating another, giving orders and getting information. I can say this quite openly because I know the Chicago Police Department doesn't want to explain why they took an order from Al Boger, Chairman of the Youth Board, to rush ten patrol cars at 4 A.M. to his home to rescue him from a band of Yippies. I also told them that Chicago was only a decoy to let us take over U.S. Steel in Gary, Indiana. It sure is one hell of a revolution.

COPS EAT PIE..... and then some

Sunday was Mothers Day: we brought apple pies to the police station, dancing, singing, in good spirits of yippie joy and celebration..,....
Everything went fine and we went back to the park and smiled at the sun and formed chains of free people and food and incense and laughter and everybody touched each other.

North Avenue Beach. Lincoln Park -- The Free Tree is born with longhair branches and naked roots. Free each sunday for all. Free tree attacks the mass paranoia fiend of the Daley slaughterhouses of death. Free type with sunlight for blossoms. Come and eat the blossoms of the free tree. Come out of the closets of your mind. FREE TREE EVERY SUNDAY.

On North Avenue the cops ambushed Paul Wadley who, stopping to help a car driven by Kitty Genovese, was grabbed and taken away in a blue and white good humor truck. People stood around and said things like "they can't do that here" or "why didn't we" and "they are simply awful" and collected 16 dollars and thirty eight cents for bail; and in general did other effective things like that as Paul was loaded aboard.

Busts are old hat. Doing nithing is old hats....
            copseatflowers   copseatflowers

Badge #9557 we don't love you anymore. No apple pie for you.

Watch your ass......

The next bust means........

                    in the streets ------

                be advised

                AL CAPONE

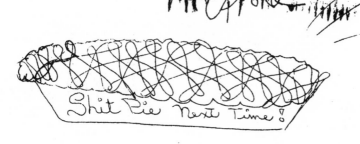

Shit Pie next Time!

SPREE — WOWEE — ARLO GUTHRIE — COLOR — GIGGLE — STREET — PLEASURE — HAPPENING — DANCING — JOY —
THE POLITICS OF ECSTASY — COUNTRY JOE AND THE FISH — BLANKETS — POETRY — SLAPSTICK — VENCEREMOS —
LIGHTS — CHALLENGE — YES — ALLEN GINSBURG — FREE — TRIBES — EXPERIENCE — ZIG-ZAG — SKULLDIGGERY —
COPSEATFLOWERS — SYMBOLS — PIPES — NOW — ABANDON THE CREEPING MEATBALL — TIMOTHY LEARY — JOY —
FLESH THEATRE — WARLOCKS — GUITARS — BELLS — HUGH ROMNEY — PEACOCK FEATHERS — PAUL KRASSNER — OM
— INNER SPACE — HELL NO WE WON'T GO — LIPS — CHERRY PIE — LIBERTY — LSD — STREAMERS — MACBIRD — VOTE
FOR ME — SUN — TURN ON — PETER MAX — PHIL OCHS — CANDLES — DRAFT BEER — MANTRAS — JOIN — GALA
MORE — DIGGERS — ROCK MUSIC — UNITED STATES OF AMERICA BAND — ENERGY — MRS. LEARY'S COW — BLOOM
— JIM FOURATT — NO CENSORSHIP — BEAUTY — KISS — NIRVANA — FLASH — SHIRLEY CLARKE — BEADS — BIRDS
— GO — BEWARE LOCAL POLICE ARMED AND CONSIDERED DANGEROUS — FOOD — GAMES — DICK GREGORY — HUG —
TENTS — LOVE — CARAVAN — WONDERFUL — FUGS — SKYDIVING — BLACKS — FREE CITY — IDEAS — TOUCH — HI!
— END ALL SYSTEMS — BARBARA TUKE — BONNIE AND CLYDE — HOPE — TRIP — DRUMS — SWEET — DRAGONS —
PURPLE — PIN THE TAIL ON THE DONKEY — PANHANDLERS — PLAN NOW — SMILE — HARI KRISHNA — TAPIOCA —
LET'S GROK — TAMBOURINES — PAUL WILLIAMS — RALLYS — NAKED — CHICKEN LITTLE — CARNIVAL — BUSES —
MONKEY — COLOR — BROTHERS — MICROBOPPERS — TOGETHER — STEVE MILLER'S BLUES BAND — VISIONS — NOW
— FREE — EXTENSION — JOHN WILCOCK — END WAR — SPIRIT — PLAY — COMMUNITY — JUDY COLLINS — FANTASY
— REALITY — ALTERNATIVE — THE WALRUS — BREAD AND PUPPET THEATRE — SWIMMING — MASKS — BUZZ — NEWS
— DELIGHT — UTEO KINO — NORMAN MAILER — GEODESIC DOMES — MEDIA — WASHINGTON FREE THEATRE — GURUS
— BANCROFT T. HOGG — FLOWERS — PAGEANT PLAYERS — SISTERS — POT — MARVIN GARSON — SINGING — FREAKOUT
— STARS — GRASS — MORE — PETER WALKER — MONKEY WARFARE — RUNAWAYS — RICHARD GOLDSTEIN — MYTH —
CHILD — BOOB — BUBBLE GUM — WATER — CHEER — GUERRILLA THEATRE — ED BERRIGAN — SHELLS — LOVERS —
WHITE LIGHTNING — FULL EMPLOYMENT — SPARKLE — LIVE — GROW — MORE — JERRY RUBIN — KITES — TUNE IN
— BOB FASS — LIGHTS — CARNIVAL — EQUALITY — HELL'S ANGELS — END MY TOILES — SMMIS — LAUGHTER —
FREE TV — BREAKOUT — TOM COTHLAMPE — BALLOONS — TOE FREAKS — BRING — JACQUES LEVY — FANFARE
— FESTIVAL — TRUCKS — ABBIE HOFFMAN — WHISTLES — MINNEAPOLIS PLAYERS — COSTUMES — NEW REELS —
UNDERGROUND NEWSPAPER — MINSTRELS — BELLY BUTTONS — MAGIC — DO — SKIN — FREE ROOMS — VITALITY —
RASCALS — SHARON KREBS — FREE AMERICA — WARMTH — FLY TRANSLOVE AIRWAYS — RESISTANCE — FROLIC — DIG
— BLOWOUT — HUG — A EINHORN — CIDER — BREEZE — ZODIAC — SPYS — HOG FARM — LIFE STYLE — MOCK
CONVENTION — BIRDS — ALAN KATZMAN — NOON — DROP-OUT — MOUTH — REBORN — REVOLUTION — LEN CHANDLER
— THE EGGMAN — SHELLS — INDIANS — LIBERATION NEWS SERVICE — THONK — MIDDLE EARTH — END PRISONS — UP
— SPEED — PAN — FREE POETRY — JAZZ — STRENGTH — RICHARD SCHECHNER — PEPPERMINT — EXCITEMENT —
PLANET — OPEN — GATHERING — SLAPSTICK — KEEP THE MAN UPTIGHT — CHOOSE — STREET — MAKE LOVE NOT
WAR — TROUBADOR — BARRICADE JUMPERS — ART — PETER GESSNER — BALL FOREVER — BORN — HAPPINESS — BOO
— BARBARA GARSON — INCENSE — LIFE — TWIRL — WITCHES — DENNIS GASTON — LEGEND — LIBERATION — FREE —
EAGER — PROP — EXALTATION — HEAVEN — MIMES — MIMICS — BONK — WING — NONSENSE — ABE PECOLICK —
BUBBLES — WINGS — GODS — DOLPHINS — STP — BURST — HEART TRANSPLANT FOR LBJ — MOVIES — BANNERS —
POPCORN — MELLOW — BREAST — NIRUMA — FUNNY — BOO HOOS — THIGH — COME — HEAD — EXPLOSION — MAU-MAU
— CLOUD — FLAME — MYSTERY — PULSE — WREN — EUCALYPTUS — SURPRISE — FLUTES — BREAD — KIWIS — SONG
— GREGORY CORSO — SMOKE — HOPSKOTCH — MARBLES — TEEPEES — KALEIDOSCOPE — STU ALBERT — ZANY —
DOGS — HAIR — SATIN — TREES — LAKES — LYSERGIC ACID CRYPTO-ETHELENE — COMMUNION — DIZZY — BLOOM —
BREATHLESS — STREAM — CONFETTI — RHYME — HARMONY — MIKE ROSSMAN — FONDLE — ROMP — FROLIC — HUG
— LEGEND — DRAMA — MYTH — REVELRY — FERIA — HIP — DELIGHT — IMPLOSION — DAY GLO — BUNKO — OPEN —
BE — ELECTRICITY — DISCOVERY — FILMS — SHARING — BANANAS — LEAFLETS — BLESSINGS — EXHILARATION —
DRUMS — THE MAN IS UPTIGHT — GOSSIMER — POSITIVE — RICE — FEATHERS — ALICE'S RESTAURANT — CANDY —
DATES — EXORCISM — ED SANDERS — SLEEP — FLY — HARMONY — EARTH — BLINK — WINK — KISS — PEACE — SEE
— DROP OUT — SOUL — DO YOUR THING — BURST — TULI KUPFERBERG — COME — TASTE — GROOVE — ACT-OUT —
DO-IN — SWING — FLOAT — HUM — SKYLARK — BELLY BUTTONS — BEAT ARMY — JOSEPH PAPP — CELEBRATE — YES
— SKETCH — RHYME — WALTER BOWART — CHALLENGE — ROMP — BELIEVE — WEAVE — PEE — GIGGLE — VIBRATE —
PAINT — CHANT — BILLY THE KID — MEDITATE — JINGLE — TANGO — CHARLIE BROWN — HURRAY — EMANCIPATE —
BLOOD, SWEAT AND TEARS — BRAIDS — STEW — CREATE — DEBATE — CANDLES — LOVERS — CYMBALS — VIOLINS —
LOLLIPOPS — GYRATE — JUBILATION — HOOKAHS — REBELS — GODDESSES — ELATION — FAITH — RADIOS — HOLY —
PHANTASMAGORIC — RABBITS — JU JUBES — PLUMES — HONEYSUCKLE — HOURIS — PARTICIPATE — GRAFFITI —
PASSION — WIZARDS — PEANUT BUTTER — LEPRECHAUNS — MIRTH — SWEAT — LINKS — PICNIC — MIMEOGRAPH —
JUVENILE EXHIBITIONISM — MARIONETTES — NATURAL — AWARDS — MOBILE — PHOENIX — LOAVES — LEVITATE —
PERFORMAL — LEAVES — MAGIC — MUTANTS — ANIMALS — OLIVES — BASEBALL — ELDEN HANDLER — OUTDOOR — ANTIC
— PETE SEEGER — AIR — FEEL — SYNCHRONICITY — TICKLE — SERENADE — SUMMER — NO MORE — INFAMY — NATIONALISM
— BALMY — SUPER — PANTOMIME — MORE — CHESTER ANDERSON — AMERICAN EXPEDITIONARY FORCE — SNATCH —
UTOPIA — PUPPIES — BEES — PEACE PIPES — QUICKSILVER — INDEPENDENCE — STRANGE — INTERGALACHO — EROS —
GET HIGH WITH A LITTLE HELP — WAVES — DANDELIONS — GROUP IMAGE — CIRCUS — TAROT DELPHI — WARPAINT —
HALOES — TOUR — RICHIE HAVENS — CONTACT — DREAM — BERRIES — GINGER — WHIZ — LICORICE — SPACESHIP
JANIS IAN — PING PONG — LOTUS BLOSSOMS — SHALOM — PIE — SPAGHETTI — GARDEN — CUCKOO — WHISPER —
ZAP — DANDY — IMAGE — PEACE EYE — DROP OUT DON'T CUP OUT — ENGAGE — TRUST — WINDMILL — ELASTIC —
FIRM — MUSHROOM — CUSHION — SIP — JIMI HENDRIX EXPERIENCE — TAKE OFF — RING — QUIXOTIC — DECLARE —
GARGLE — FACE — PEACH — MARTIN JEZER — PEPPERMINT — INTERNATIONAL — VIVID — COMMUNITY — DANCING
★ ★ YOUTH INTERNATIONAL PARTY — 32 UNION SQUARE, ROOM 607, NEW YORK, N. Y. 10003 — (212) 982-5090 ★ ★

YI PYIPYIPYIYPYIPYIPYIPYIPYIPYIPYIPYIPYIPYIPYIPYIPIEEEEEEEEEEEEEEEEAUM

Impartial List of Delegate Housings

State (/!?)   Location al Co-ordinates

Tennessee   Rm #11, (3rd floor) Palmer House, State & Monroe Streets
                       Rm #14, (Club for)   RA 6-7500
Alabama   Parlor B
South Carolina   Rm #6, (3rd floor)
New Jersey   Rm #5, (3rd floor)
Florida   Rm #17, (Club floor)
New Mexico   dRm #7&8 (3rd floor)
Massachuttess (Massachuttesses?) Rm#9, (3rd floor)

New York   11th Floor, Exhibition Hall (meetings)
                       Sheraton Chicago Hotel (housing), 505 N. MIchigan
                                                           WA 4-4100
California   18th floor, La Salle Hotel (housing)
                       Rooms J, K, L (Mezzanine floor for meetings)
Missouri   La Salle Hotle tenative housing

Pennsylvania   Shermann House (Randolph caucausses, street level)
  oHIo   smae as Penn (Bal. Taberin caucausses, 6th floor)
Illinoise (Li La La La!) same as Penn. and oHIo (crystal & Louis XIV Rooms, 1st floor)
                       Clark & Randolph Streets, FR2-2100

BREAK-IN BREAK-IN BREAK-IN Break-it-in BREAK-IN BREAK-IN BREAK-IN BREAK-IN
   Security precautions taken by convention big-wigs are a farce. Emergencies do happen
and we're all actors in the play of life. Bill Roberts is the assistant to Bill Henry, who is
the Charman (chair-man?), 1968 Political Cov. Raddo & teevee Committee in Washington.
Tom Jarriel is on general assignment for ABC. ABC is housed at the Ambassador, the
Astor Tower, the Drake, Mid-America Inn, Oxford House Motor Hotel and Seneca Hotel.

FREAK FREAK FREAK FREAK FREAK FREAK FREAK FREAK FREAK FREAK DO IT!
          OHM AUM OH HO HO HO HE HE HA HA HA
ACTION SITES
City Hall - Washinton & Clark Sts.   Electric Theater - 4812 N. Clark 784-1700
Police HQ - 1121 S. State Street   Induction Center - 615 W. Van Burien
Mayor Daley's pad - 3536 S. Lowe   Knickerbocker Hotel- 163 E Walton
Cultural Exploiters -   Pick-Congress Hotel - Congress Parkway
Cheetah-Aragon Ballroom- 1106 W. Lawr. 561-8558   & Michigan Streets

BUY THE RAT SELL THE SEED SELL THE RAT BUY THE SEED BUY SELL SELL BUY
MONEY MONEY MONEY MONEY MONEY MONEY MONEY MONEY INFORMATION

NOTE: Dear reader, detailed maps of the Chicago loop showing locations and delegate info
can be found in the Convention Special issue of RAT. Get it. Seed phone mutuality listing is
337-2623 337-2623. YIPPIE telecommunication center contact co-ordinates: 943-5282.
We need chicks who can type (and spell), cats who have wheels and want to do a Digger trip
to feed the masses (when they finally decide that this is where it's happening). Come with us.

          WARNING... LOCAL COPS ARE ARMED AND CONSIDERED DANGEROUS!!!!

"BE REALISTIC, DEMAND THE IMPOSSIBLE."

Slogan on a Paris wall during the Student Rebellion

REVOLUTION TOWARDS A FREE SOCIETY: YIPPIE! *

By A. Yippie

1. An immediate end to the War in Vietnam and a restructuring of our foreign policy which totally eliminates aspects of military, economic, and cultural imperialism. The withdrawal of all foreign based troops and the abolition of the military draft.

2. Immediate freedom for Huey Newton of the Black Panthers and all other black people. Adoption of the community control concept in our ghetto areas. An end to the cultural and economic domination of minority groups.

3. The legalization of marihuana and all other psychedelic drugs. The freeing of all prisoners currently in prison on narcotics charges.

4. A prison system based on the concept of rehabilitation rather than punishment.

5. A judicial system which works toward the abolition of all laws related to crimes without victims. That is, retention only of laws relating to crimes in which there is an unwilling injured party, i. e. murder, rape, assault.

6. The total disarmament of all the people beginning with the police. This includes not only guns, but such brutal devices as tear gas, MACE, electric prods, blackjacks, billy clubs, and the like.

7. The Abolition of Money. The abolition of pay housing, pay media, pay transportation, pay food, pay education, pay clothing, pay medical help, and pay toilets.

8. A society which works toward and actively promotes the concept of "full-unemployment." A society in which people are free from the drudgery of work. Adoption of the concept "Let the Machines do it."

* This is a personal statement. There are no spokesmen for the Yippies. We suggest to all reporters that they ask each and every Yippie in Lincoln Park why they have come to Chicago. We are all our own leaders. We realize this list of demands is inconclusive, they are not really demands. For people to make demands of the Democratic Party is an exercise in wasted wish-fulfillment. If we have a demand it is simply and emphatically that they, along with their fellow inmates in the Republican Party cease to exist. We demand a society built along the alternative community in Lincoln Park, a society based on humanitarian cooperation and equality, a society which allows and promotes the creativity present in all people and especially our youth.

(OVER)

9. A conservation program geared towards preserving our natural resources and committed to the elimination of pollution from our air and water.

10. A program of ecological development that will provide incentives for the decentralization of our crowded cities and encourage rural living.

11. A program which provides not only free birth control information and devices but also abortions when desired.

12. A restructured educational system which provides the student power to determine his course of study and allows for student participation in over-all policy planning. Also an educational system which breaks down its barriers between school and community. A system which uses the surrounding community as a classroom so that students may learn directly the problems of the people.

13. The open and free use of the media. A program which actively supports and promotes cable television as a method of increasing the selection of channels available to the viewer.

14. An end to all censorship. We are sick of a society which has no hesitation about showing people committing violence and refuses to show a couple fucking.

15. We believe that people should fuck all the time, anytime, whomever they wish. This is not a program demand but a simple recognition of the reality around us.

16. A political system which is more streamlined and responsive to the needs of all the people regardless of age, sex or race. Perhaps a national referendum system conducted via television or a telephone voting system. Perhaps a decentralization of power and authority with many varied tribal groups. Groups in which people exist in a state of basic trust and are free to choose their tribe.

17. A program that encourages and promotes the arts. However, we feel that if the Free Society we envision were to be fought for and achieved, all of us would actualize the creativity within us. In a very real sense we would have a society in which every man would be an artist.

18.

* *

It is for these reasons that we have come to Chicago. It is for these reasons that many of us may fight and die here. We recognize this as the vision of the founders of this nation. We recognize that we are America. We recognize that we are Free Men. The present day politicians and their armies of automatons have selfishly robbed us of our birthright. The evilness they stand for will go unchallenged no longer. Political Pigs, your days are numbered. We are the Second American Revolution. We shall win. Yippie!

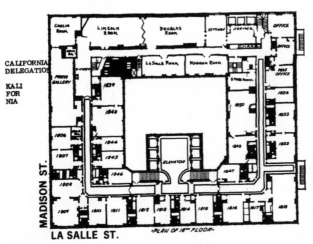

LA SALLE

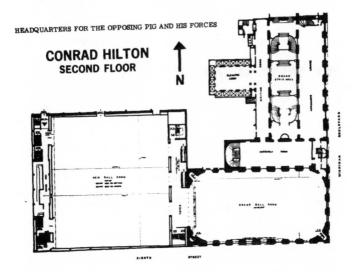

HEADQUARTERS FOR THE OPPOSING PIG AND HIS FORCES

CONRAD HILTON
SECOND FLOOR

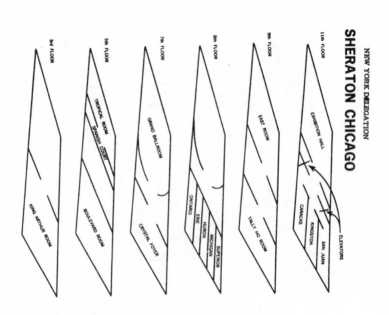

SHERATON CHICAGO

NEW YORK DELEGATION

11th FLOOR — EXHIBITION HALL, CARACAS, KINGSTON, SAN JUAN, ELEVATORS

9th FLOOR — EAST ROOM, TALLY HO ROOM

8th FLOOR — ONTARIO, ERIE, HURON, MICHIGAN, SUPERIOR

7th FLOOR — GRAND BALLROOM, CRYSTAL FOYER

5th FLOOR — TROPICAL ROOM, SPANISH COURT, BOULEVARD ROOM

3rd FLOOR — KING ARTHUR ROOM

GATHERING PLACE FOR THE TEAR IT DOWN TOWN MEETING OF THE WORLD

INTERNATIONAL AMPHITHEATRE

 ← N

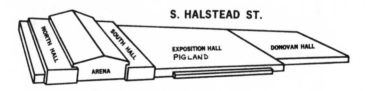

S. HALSTEAD ST.

NORTH HALL, SOUTH HALL, ARENA, EXPOSITION HALL PIGLAND, DONOVAN HALL

DEXTER PARK AVE.

Youth International Party
837 N. LaSalle

SWIMMING - SWIMMING

DARING ESPOSE--TOP SECRET YIPPIE PLANS for LINCOLN PARK

"Lincoln Park...God's enchanting acres named in grateful remembrance of the Great Emancipator, once the hallowed grounds of many of the city's departed pioneers...now the wonder spot of the Midwest, the playground of millions."

Chicago Tourist Bureau

August 20-August 24 (AM)--------Training in snake dancing, karate, non-violent self-defense. Information booth in Park.
August 24 (PM)------------------Yippie Mayor R. Daley presents fireworks on Lake Michigan.
August 25 (AM)------------------Welcoming of the Democratic delegates--downtown hotels(to be announced).
August 25 (PM)------------------MUSIC FESTIVAL--Lincoln Park
August 26 (AM)------------------Workshop in drug problems, underground communications, how to live free, guerrilla theatre, self-defense, draft resistance, communes, etc. (Potential workshop leaders should call the Seed, 837 N. LaSalle Street, 943 5282).
Scenario sessions to plan small group activities.
August 26 (PM)---------------Beach Party ON THE LAKE ACROSS from Lincoln Park (North Avenue Beach)
-----folksinging, barbecues, swimming, lovemaking

August 27 (dawn)--------------Poetry, mantras, religious ceremony.
August 27 (AM)---------------Workshops and Scenario sessions.
Film showing and mixed media--Coliseum
August 27 (PM)---------------Benefit concert--Coliseum 1513 S. Wabash
Rally and Nomination of Pigasus and LBJ birthday party--Lincoln Park.
August 28 (dawn)--------------Poetry and Folk singing
August 28 (AM)----------------Yippie Olympics, Miss Yippie Contest, catch the candidate, pin the tale on the donkey, pin the rubber on the Pope, and other normal, healthy games.
August 28 (PM)----------------Plans to be announced at a later date.
4 P.M.--Mobilization Rally scheduled for Grant Park. March to the Convention.
August 29-30------------------Events scheduled depend on Wed. nite. Return to park for sleeping.

DIRECTIONS TO LINCOLN PARK

Subway-----Jackson Pk. or Englewood trains to Clark and Division (1200 n) walk north on Clark to the park.
Bus---------Wilson-LaSalle (156) to Inner Drive and North Avenue.
Wilson-Michigan to LaSalle Drive and North Avenue.
Clark Street (22) to Clark and North.
Broadway 36 to Clark and Wisconsin (1800)
Lincoln-Wabash to Lincoln and Wells (1800 n.)
Armitage-Odgen to Armitage and Wells (1900 N.)
North Avenue bus east to North and LaSalle.
Car--------north or south on Lake Shore Drive to North Avenue exit. west on North avenue.
Raft--------St. Lawrence Seaway to Lake Michigan--head south.

near Old Town
Chicago's Village

forty foot totem pole

picnic facilities
near zoo

contact 943-5282 for Yippie information.

PROPS CAN BE STORED AT THE THEATRE 1846 NORTH WELLS - ACROSS FROM LINCOLN PARK

SWIMMING - SWIMMING

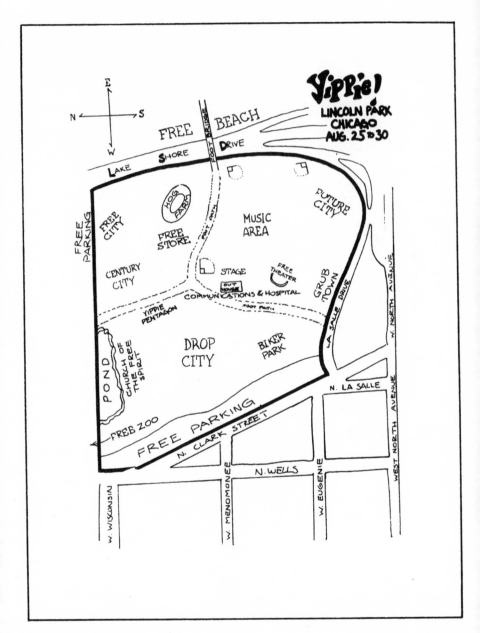

9

EXTRA QUOTES, BITS & PIECES

Now we have some interesting quotations to lend a certain respectability to the book. There are also bits and pieces of garbage that you can add or discard. You can cut along the lines and paste them where you feel comfortable. If you want to read the books you have to look for them. I would have liked to include excerpts from rock music but unfortunately my record player is broken. I would have also used parts of Norman Mailer's brilliant book *Armies of the Night* but I gave my copy away. Here, as always, the principle is *Use what you have available.* I can think of three *M*'s that would prove very helpful. The first two were my teachers at Brandeis, the third I've never met but I watch him on television.

MASLOW
    MARCUSE
        McLUHAN

                Then of course there are the
                Marx Brothers, Karl included.

The only way out of the dilemma of our society is to say that in the short run, everyone is entitled to a guaranteed income — and this is the very short run, and then very rapidly move into a society in which you simply go into a store and take what you want.

        — ROBERT THEOBALD, Los Angeles *Free Press,*
        September 29, 1967

Learning karate on the run. Pick up a move here, a move there. Practicing on the streets. I tried to close down this bad news commune on 11th Street run by Spade Charlie, a real amphetamine, V.D., clap headquarters. I stormed in the door screaming "Clean the place up." I gave some girl huddled in the corner two dollars and told her to go home. Spade Charlie, 250 pounds of blubber, dropped his amphetamine snort and picked up a bread knife in a rage. "Who said that?" "I did, motherfucker." It worked. He backed down.

Little guy'll whop a big guy every time long as the little guy's
in the right and keeps a cummin.

— TERRY SOUTHERN, *The Magic Christian*
(Motto of the Texas Rangers)

Two days in New Hampshire at Marty's. LSD naked in the
woods. God it was beautiful. We lost our suitcase on the bus
coming back because we got out at Hartford to get a cup of
coffee and the bus left without us. There we were, Anita and I,
in the middle of Hartford's downtown slum area at 3 A.M. on
Sunday. Some black crazy cat threw a cup of coffee at a white
drunk and rolled him. I talked to him for awhile about SNCC
while the drunk kept weaving around yelling for a cop. The
mugger was cool as all hell, a real killer type.

Do you know people were calling up the TV station in Detroit
during the riots, asking if their neighborhood was being attacked. That's where most of scared white America is. Afraid to
even look out the window, so alienated they don't even know
where their neighborhood is anymore.

Saw a Ford Motor commercial last month that began "In the old
days when there were men and Indians. . . ." Isn't that unbelievable! It's hard to keep your cool in this land of the free . . .
eechs! The land that Columbus discovered (?) — what does
that mean anyway, seeing as how there were people living here
for quite some time.

Poets don't count in this country . . . that's why they are so free
of course. Artistic freedom is really an insult here. Take Russia
or an East European country like Poland — they are scared shitless of poets. That's why they ban a lot of anti-government stuff
— because they respect a poet's power. Can you imagine the
U.S. government trying to buy off Allen Ginsberg? Only when
they go abroad does that happen, because people out there,
those foreign kooks, listen to poets. Here in the U.S.A. they

don't care what poets say 'cause nobody listens to them anyway. Poet revolutionaries are the most dangerous of all.

As long as there are no myths accepted by the masses, one may go on talking of revolts indefinitely, without ever provoking any revolutionary movement.

— GEORGE SOREL, *Reflections on Violence*

Now I ask you: What can be expected of man since he is a being endowed with such strange qualities? Shower upon him every earthly blessing, drown him in a sea of happiness, so that nothing but bubbles of bliss can be seen on the surface; give him economic prosperity such that he should have nothing else to do but sleep, eat cakes and busy himself with the continuation of his species, and even then out of sheer ingratitude, sheer spite, man would play you some nasty trick. He would even risk his cakes and would deliberately desire the most fatal rubbish, the most uneconomical absurdity, simply to introduce into all this positive good sense his fatal fantastic element. It is just his fantastic dreams, his vulgar folly, that he will desire to retain, simply in order to prove to himself — as though that were so necessary — that men still are men and not the keys of a piano, which the laws of nature threaten to control so completely that soon one will be able to desire nothing but by the calendar. And that is not all: even if man really were nothing but a piano key, even if this were proved to him by natural science and mathematics, even then he would not become reasonable, but would purposely do something perverse out of simple ingratitude, simply to gain his point. And if he does not find means he will contrive destruction and chaos, will contrive sufferings of all sorts, only to gain his point! He will launch a curse upon the world, and as only man can curse (it is his privilege, the primary distinction between him and other animals) it may be by his curse alone he will attain his object — that is, convince himself that he is a man and not a piano key!

— FYODOR DOSTOYEVSKY, *Notes from Underground*

It is up to us to create God. He is not the creator. That is the whole history of Christianity. For we have but one way of creating God, which is to become Him.

— CAMUS, *Notebooks 1942–1951*

On his first missionary visit to Antioch in Asia Minor, the apostle Paul and those with him found many persons that were unreceptive to the good news that they preached. They were even mobbed out of town by these people, but this unpleasant experience did not cause them to develop the wrong mental attitude toward their work and thus cause it to lose its joy.

— Acts 13:52 as interpreted by *The Watchtower*

This country with its constitution belongs to those who live in it. Whenever they shall grow weary of the existing government they shall exercise their constitutional rights of amending it or their revolutionary right to dismember or overthrow it.

— ABRAHAM LINCOLN

The other day somebody gave me a picture book called *This America* by Lyndon Baines Johnson. Can you imagine fucking up a picture book — a book like, say, *Family of Man* or *Personally Yours?* Impossible, hm? But not for Lyndon. The very first photo — two full pages — is a black and white, desolate landscape, looks like the other side of the moon, cold, sterile, not a living, breathing thing. The caption reads: "For this is what America is all about."

INTERVIEWER: Mr. Shankar, what do you think of all the swamis running around New York?
RAVI SHANKAR: Well, I hope they're not all phonies. There are a lot of phony swamis in India.

My girl and I went up to the U.N. today to watch the debate. After a while it seemed so ridiculous and disgusting, my girl and I began to make love in the gallery. They threw us out but

I still think what we were doing was more valid than what those clowns were into.

— TEENAGER on WBAI-FM

When sheep walk into the den of the wolves they should be as harmless as doves and as cunning as snakes.

— JESUS

Observe how many poor hands and how many good hands show up; this will give you an idea of what to expect other players to hold in an actual game. Learn the rules on various poker games and get advice from skillful players. Most important of all, play poker in actual games. No amount of study compares with actual play for learning a game.

— ALBERT MOREHEAD, *How to Become a Good Poker Player*

The man who owned the bookstore was not magic. He was not a three-legged crow on the dandelion side of the mountain.

— RICHARD BRAUTIGAN, *Trout Fishing in America*
(I don't know where this fits but I loved the book)

There is a brilliant dialogue sequence in the Beatles' *Hard Day's Night*. Remember the scene with the Beatles jumping around a grassy lot playing all sorts of games. A very tough landlord type appears.

LANDLORD: You know this is private property, don't you?
BEATLES: Ah, we just wanted to have a little fun.

The revolution as myth is the definitive revolution.

— CAMUS, *Notebooks 1942–1951*

ALICE: Yes, but where do I begin?
CHESHIRE CAT: Why, my dear, you begin at the beginning.

— LEWIS CARROLL, *Alice in Wonderland*

Everything derives from the fact that those who have the responsibility of speaking for the masses don't have, never have, a real concern for liberty.

— CAMUS, *Notebooks 1942–1951*

Can the individual choose the moment when he can die for truth?

— PARAIN

The idea that no solution exists never occurs to them and in this lies their strength.

— RENAN

Once when Rabbi Pinhas entered the house of study, he saw that his disciples, who had been talking busily, stopped and stared at his coming. He asked them: "What were you talking about?"

"Rabbi," they said, "We were saying how afraid we are that the Evil Urge will pursue us."

"Don't worry," he replied. "You have not gotten high enough for it to pursue you. For the time being you are still pursuing it."

— MARTIN BUBER, *Tales of Hassidim*

I have doubts about today and about ourselves. You would laugh, Dario, if I told you this aloud. You would say, spreading your great shaggy, brotherly, strong hands: "Me, I feel able to win all the way. All the way." This is how we all feel, immortal, right up to the moment when we feel nothing at all anymore. And life goes on after our little drop of water has flowed back into the ocean. In this sense my confidence is one with yours. Tomorrow is great. We will not have prepared this conquest in vain. The city will be won, if not by our hands, at least by hands like ours, only stronger; perhaps stronger by being better toughened through our very weakness. If we are beaten, other men infinitely like us will come down this ramble on an evening like this, in ten years, twenty years, it matters not, planning the same conquest. Perhaps they will be thinking of the blood we shed; more likely not. Even now I think I can see them. I am thinking of their blood which will also flow. But they will win the city.

— VICTOR SERGE, *Memoirs of a Revolutionary*

Freedom will cure most things.

— A. S. NEILL, *Summerhill*

A PSYCHOLOGICAL UTOPIA

... this would almost surely be a highly anarchistic group, a laissez-faire but loving culture, in which people (young people too) would have much more free choice than we are used to, and in which wishes would be respected much more than they are in our society. People would not bother each other so much as we do, would be much less prone to press opinions or religions or philosophies or tastes in clothes or food or art or women on their neighbors. In a word, the inhabitants of Eupsychia would tend to be permissive, wish-respecting and gratifying (whenever possible), would frustrate only under certain conditions that I have not attempted to describe, and would permit people to make free choices wherever possible. Under such conditions, the deepest layers of human nature could show themselves with great ease.

— MASLOW, *Motivation and Personality*

Whereas in the mechanical age of fragmentation leisure had been the absence of work, or mere idleness, the reverse is true in the electric age. As the age of information demands the simultaneous use of all our faculties, we discover that we are most at leisure when we are most intensely involved, very much as with the artists in all ages.

— MARSHALL MCLUHAN, in Robert Theobald,
The Guaranteed Income

What we call "jobs" represent a relatively recent pattern of work. When a man is using all his faculties we think he is at leisure or at play. The artist doesn't have a job because he uses

all his powers at once. Were he to pause to work out his income
tax, he would be using only a few of his powers. That would be
a "job." A mother doesn't have a "job" because she has to do
forty jobs at once. So with a top executive or surgeon. Under
conditions of electric circuitry all the fragmented job patterns
tend to blend once more into involving and demanding forms of
work that more and more resemble teaching and learning and
"human service" in its older sense of dedicated loyalty.

— McLuhan in *The Guaranteed Income*

The headline of the *Daily News* today reads BRUNETTE
STABBED TO DEATH. Underneath in lower case letters:
"6,000 Killed in Iranian Earthquake"... I wonder what color
hair they had?

What happened in Chicago can be viewed in terms of a game.
Football serves as the best model. (See McLuhan's *Understanding Media* and Norman Mailer's discussion of the Single Wing
vs. the T-formation in his book *Advertisements for Myself*.) Cops
vs. Yippies, YIP vs. MOB, Cops vs. Newsmen, Newsmen vs. Yippies. I would have loved to see the headline "Cops vs. National
Guard." My money would have been on the Guard. One night in
Chicago I heard part of a live broadcast of a football game. "The
guards smashed through the center, Taylor is now running
around end, he's really flying — SMASH! They nailed him good.
It's a fumble . . ." I listened for about two minutes before I
realized it wasn't the Battle of Michigan Avenue they were
describing.

The only things I own are my boots and a silver wedding ring.
Anita bought me a portable tape recorder for our wedding. A
month later I gave the tape recorder to Tom Hayden during
the Newark Revolt when we brought over the truckloads of
food. Anita never said a word. In a way, I guess we still
have it.

Once in Japan there existed a group of warriors called the "No-
Swordsmen." A Samurai and a No-Swordsman were riding on a

raft with some people when the Samurai challenged the No-Swordsman to a duel. The No-Swordsman replied, "Let's jump out when we get to the next island rather than fight on the raft and possibly hurt the others." When the raft drifted by an island, the Samurai jumped out. The No-Swordsman didn't and the raft moved on. I wonder who won the duel? Funny about the word "duel," if you change one letter it becomes "duet."

And so you ask, "What about the innocent bystanders?" But we are in a time of revolution. If you are a bystander, you are not innocent.

When can I go into the Super Market and buy what I need with my good looks?

— ALLEN GINSBERG, "America"

Guerrilla theater is only a transitional step in the development of total life-actors. Life-actors never rehearse and need no script. *A life-actor uses whatever he has available*, nothing more, nothing less.

Guns are an interesting prop. Five months ago I got my first gun from a Hell's Angel friend. It was a 22-caliber pearlhandled pistol. I shot it into the wall of my living room. It made a hell of a racket. I kept it loaded under the bureau. When Jerry got busted I got rid of it along with the dope, fireworks, fuses, and various other assorted props. Although I admire the revolutionary art of the Black Panthers, I feel guns alone will never change this System. You don't use a gun on an IBM computer. You pull the plug out.

A Yippie believes only what he sees with his own two eyes, he accepts the rest as bullshit. A Yippie should examine his eyes once a month.

We are the people our parents warned us against.

— NICK VON HOFFMAN

> Choose your weapons
> Guns or Flowers.
> Flowers shoot rotten bullets,
> Guns make lousy flower pots.
>
> — A famous Digger poem

(Highly recommended is *The Digger Papers,* a collection of Digger shit passed out free in Free City. We love you Emmett wherever you are.)

TODAY IS THE FIRST DAY OF THE REST OF YOUR LIFE

The best way to educate oneself is to become part of the revolution.

> — CHÉ GUEVARA

On the Friday before the Sunday, with "borrowed" *Life* Magazine credentials I got into the International Amphitheater. I was stunned by the contrast between their stage and ours in Lincoln Park. The art work was by Howard Johnson, it had an unbelievable smell of decay and shit. (I read in *Time* Magazine that speakers at the podium had to be sprayed to keep away flies that were attracted by two huge manure piles next to the Convention.)

*   *   *   *

The Lord of the Flies hung on the stick like a black ball . . . The flies had found the figure too. The little life movement would scare them off for a moment so that they made a dark cloud round the head. Then as the blue material of the parachute collapsed the corpulent figure would bow forward, sighing, and the flies settle once more.

> — WILLIAM GOLDING, *Lord of the Flies*

One night before it all happened I rode out to Bridgeport to see where Mayor Daley lived. It was a simple, sturdy bungalow no different from the others on the block, except for the guards. On the corner of the block, not fifty feet from Daley's house, was a huge, dull building with a sign over the door that said POLICE HEADQUARTERS. After seeing the rugged way he lived, there was no doubt in my mind that we would ever get a permit for anything.

AYippie
    is a hippie who's beenbusted
    is a p a i d assassin
    has permanent chro mo so me   damage
    has bad breath
    hasno   problems
    hasno   underwear
    hasno   money
    never   asks what'shappening
    never sleeps
    i s a l m o s t a l w a y s f u l l o f s h i t .

This Book is dedicated to:
all the buffalo imprisoned
    in concentration camps
in San Francisco
    and throughout America
It is also dedicated
    to the proposition
that it is the obligation
    of all free men and women
to do all they can to free
    those buffalo
wirecutters cost $1.98
    they could be your last purchase.

                — CHARLES PERKEL, The Buffalo Man,
                             Buffalo City

One of my favorite quotes appeared in the Chicago *Tribune* on the Thursday before the Sunday: "According to Colonel Jack Reilley, the man chiefly responsible for the defense and security of Chicago and the Convention, there are no groups planning demonstrations during Convention Week."

THE PROBLEM IS NOT WHAT TO DO IN THE REVOLUTION BUT WHAT TO DO IN-BETWEEN THE REVOLUTION.

Remembering about how you won the Battle of Chicago is not going to win the war.

Prediction: Because of our actions in Chicago, Richard Nixon will be elected President. Furthermore, Nixon will end the war in Vietnam. He will not only have a better chance than Humphrey but even than McCarthy of achieving a solution. Nixon will find it easier to deal with the National Liberation Front in Vietnam than to deal with the American Liberation Front here at home.

A month ago I interviewed the three heads of Youth for Wallace in Wallace's New York Headquarters in Queens. I like Wallace, he is a true American. The opening of the interview went like this:

ME: How many niggers work in the campaign?
THEM: *(climbing the walls)* We don't use that word!
ME: *(naïvely)* What word?
THEM: Nigger.
ME: What do you say?
THEM: *(in unison)* Knee-Grow, Knee-Grow, Knee-Grow, Knee-Grow . . .
I sort of wish they hadn't practiced on me.

We present America with her most difficult problem. For America to burn innocent countries abroad is no problem, for America to commit genocide on the blacks that live in her cellar is no problem, for America to kill her children, that is her most difficult problem.

We have often been accused of being media-oriented. As with all criticism, it is both true and not true. The Mobilization had five times the number of press conferences that we did but we received five times the amount of coverage. The impression that we are media freaks is created by our ability to make news. *MEDIA is Communication.* The concept of getting it all out there applies whether you are speaking to one person or two hundred million.

We are printing 20,000 buttons that say YIPPIE! LEADER.

I believe in compulsory cannibalism. If people were forced to eat what they killed, there would be no more wars.

I read in the New York *Post* today that my bail bond has been increased to $5,000 and a warrant issued for my arrest — all this because of a naughty four-letter word. The honkie that tried to kill me, with an unregistered, loaded pistol, was held only three hours and released on $300 bail. I guess America is getting more prepared for guns than fucking.

The Street has always been an intriguing symbol in middle-class American life. It was always the place to avoid. There is "violence in the streets," "bad people in the streets," and "danger in the streets." It was always "let's keep the kids off the streets" as honkie America rushed from inside to inside. It is in the streets that we will make our struggle. The streets belong to the people! Long live the flower-cong of the gutters!

The FBI visited me this morning. As usual I bummed cigarettes, breakfast, and information. I found out they were having a difficult time proving conspiracy charges because of the Chicago police's mishandling of the situation. I also discovered their names, the fact that they have my phone tapped, and other valuable information. I told them I needed $20,000 to help me get to Prague, and inquired why they never asked if I was clubbed by cops, which is what the papers said they were investigating. I gave them an analysis of J. Edgar Hoover's latent homosexuality and other important information. Never be afraid to talk to your enemy. If you are good you

can always find out more about them than they can about you.
If you are not good keep your mouth shut. When the FBI
visits you they already know the answers to the questions anyway. Never attribute more intelligence to your enemy than to
yourself and your brothers. Always trust your brothers and
yourself.

The only persons who should use the word "we" are kings, editors and people with tapeworms.

— MARK TWAIN

THE ONLY WAY TO SUPPORT A REVOLUTION IS TO MAKE YOUR OWN.

Catch-22 says they have a right to do anything we can't stop
them from doing.

— JOSEPH HELLER, Catch-22

THE GROUND YOU ARE STANDING ON IS A LIBERATED ZONE, DEFEND IT.

I have just visited the future. One cannot really talk of revolution without visiting "Man and his World" (formerly Expo '67)
in Montreal. It is fantastic on a weekday morning when there
are few tourists. It's magic to walk the mahogany boardwalks,
ride streamlined tramways and flashing escalators. All Day-glos,
purples, pinks, and greens. Twisting copper cobwebs, stretches
of steel pillars, flowing concrete wings, and plastic tunnels.
Cubes, triangles, bubbles, spaghetti nets, circles of light, foun-
tains of energy; these are the shapes of things to come. One
cannot tell the church from the fun house. "Is this the roller
coaster or the subway, sir?" It is a perfect blend of harmony
and excitement. I watched the people carefully as they laughed
and danced through Future City . . . No one threw his garbage
on the floor.

job with another steel concern. *NY 3/15/68*

Poll of Democrats Finds Many Hawks Backed McCarthy

A poll of Democratic voters in New-Hampshire before the Presidential primary Tuesday showed that more than half those interviewed did not know where Senator Eugene J. McCarthy stood on the Vietnam war.

The poll also indicated that the more the voters knew the Minnesota Democrat was a dove on the war, the less likely they were to vote for him.

Senator McCarthy received about 42 per cent of the primary vote and, according to an analysis of the earlier survey, many of these votes came from people who were hawks on the war.

The sampling of Democratic primary voters was conducted throughout New Hampshire on Feb. 23 and 24 when 300 voters were interviewed by Oliver Quayle & Co., Inc., a public opinion survey company in Bronxville, N. Y. The survey was made for the National Broadcasting Company.

Both N.B.C. and the survey company concluded that the Democratic vote in New Hampshire was a vote of dissatisfaction with the Vietnam war but not a vote for a dovish stand.

N.B.C. said it believed the heavy vote for Senator McCarthy was not a vote against President Johnson's Vietnam policy but against Mr. Johnson himself.

The President received about 48 per cent of the vote in a write-in campaign.

The image
    is
        more
            involving
than the issue.

Gunman Is Laughed Off

PORTSMOUTH, N. H. (AP) —A gunman walked into a small store last night, announced it was a holdup, and ordered five customers to lie on the floor. The customers laughed. The gunman fled without any loot.

NY Post 2/23/68

PPORTUNITIES   Bus

We will defend ourselves by any means necessary.

Abbie the Loony Bird Is Brought Low by a Hunter

BY JACK SMITH

LOS ANGELES—The merry adventures of Abbie the madcap hornbill have come to a sad end.

Abbie is dead—killed in the full bloom of nubile youth by an unknown hunter.

For Abbie, who had yet to be mated to the only other African Hornbill at the Los Angeles Zoo, it was a case of too much too soon.

The big bird's body was found Friday night near a gas station in the Newhall area. She had been missing from the zoo since Jan. 25.

Her untimely end left her intended mate without hope. There are no other female hornbills at the zoo, and all too few in Africa.

Seen at Race Track

Since she flew her coop three weeks ago, she had covered a vast area, apparently enjoying her freedom and foraging off the land.

She was first spotted Jan. 29 at Hollywood Park race track, trying to move in on the swans

in the infield lake. Frank Todd, assistant curator of birds, led two keepers in a slapstick chase around the park, but Abbie got away.

Two days later she made a leisurely but skittish tour of the downtown area, pursed only by a photographer.

Last Thursday Abbie turned up in suburban Reseda. She was in a eucalyptus tree. Frank Todd rushed out again. He chased the wild girl all over the Reseda area, but finally she tired of the sport and made

for the hills to the northwest. Apparently she encountered a malicious hunter, or an innocent citizen who might understandably have been frightened by her 5-foot wingspread and awesome beak.

She Put on a Show

While she was free, though, Abbie had given the entire metropolis a bit of fun. The zoo received perhaps 1,000 phone calls from citizens who saw her, or thought they did.

Los Angeles Times-Washington Post

Everything is News.

Bulletproof Glass Encloses Gallery At Stock Exchange

NYT 11/27/69

The New York Stock Exchange last night installed bulletproof glass panels and a metal grillwork ceiling on its visitors' gallery for what an exchange spokesman said were "reasons of security."

It is the first time since the gallery was opened to the public in 1938 that any barrier—except for a three-and-one-half-foot railing—has been erected between visitors and the traders on the floor 15 feet below.

Work to enclose the 100-foot-long gallery, which in places hangs directly over the desks and telephone booths of clerks and brokers, began shortly after the close of trading at 3:30 P.M. yesterday. The job was expected to be completed before today's 10 A.M. opening bell.

The glass panels will shut off to visitors most of the frantic roar from the floor, and the grillwork will prevent, the exchange hopes, any visitor from "accidentally or on purpose" tossing things on the traders.

Last Aug. 24 a dozen or so hippies threw dollar bills from the gallery—a display many exchange members do not want to see repeated.

Officials at the exchange recall no incident of objects any heavier than dollar bills being dropped or tossed from the gallery. "But there is always a chance of it," an exchange spokesman said.

Officials would not comment on why a bulletproof partition was ordered.

According to a spokesman for David Shuldiner, Inc., the contractors who installed the panels, the glass is one and three sixteenth inches thick and laminated with plastic sheets to stop a bullet from almost any side arm.

MYTHS HAVE MORE POWER THAN REALITY.

One night in Chicago I called David Stahl, Deputy Mayor. "Dave, I just read that you have all these troops guarding reservoirs and water filtration plants against LSD. I guess you did see *Wild in the Streets*, huh? I'll give you two secrets. First, we never started that rumor and second, it can't be done. Why don't you ask your scientists? You must have some on the payroll."

Stahl responded, "We aren't taking any chances, anyway,"

The troops are still out there, probably.

2 Officers Wounded   *Miami Herald*
12/27/67

Naked, Sword-Waving Youth Shot by Police

SUNNYVALE, Calif. — (AP) — A naked youth who may have been suffering a drug reaction was shot dead in the street after attacking a policeman with a sword here Christmas afternoon. Another policeman was accidentally shot in the bizarre incident.

Killed was Daniel Bruce Brown, 19, who lived with his parents. Mr. and Mrs. Thomas Brown told authorities their son had taken LSD previously but that they didn't know if he had taken any before he sallied forth naked, brandishing a curved 40-inch sword.

Police said officers James Brice and Richard Malvini answered a call a block from Brown's home and each rolled up his squad car window when the nude Brown whacked the front of their cars with his sword.

When a third officer, Lt. G. W. Rake, arrived, Brice and Malvini got out of their cars and began to close in on Brown on foot.

Unlike Brice and Malvini, Rake left his window down as he tried to talk to Brown. Brown thrust his sword at Rake, who jumped out the other door.

Brown then turned to Malvini, who was yelling at the swordsman to stop. Brown advanced on Malvini, who backed away from him, and stumbled backward over a small lawn fence.

From his supine position he shouted at Brown once more. Brown lunged at him with the sword, nicking his knee.

Malvini fired a warning shot, and as Brown kept coming he fired four more times. Three bullets hit Brown, felling him. One bullet hit Brice in the side.

Brown was dead on arrival at a hospital, where Brice was reported in good condition with his gunshot wound. Malvinia's sword wound was treated and he was discharged.

N.Y. TIMES 10/5/67

Army Demonstrates Riot Control Tactics

FORT BELVOIR, Va., Oct. 4 (AP)—The Army demonstrated today its latest riot control tactics and equipment.

The setting was Riotsville, U.S.A., a mockup of a city area swept by disorder.

While about 3,000 persons observed from bleachers, a Riotsville mob made up of soldiers dressed as hippies set fire to buildings, overturned two cars and looted stores.

Then, with bayonets fixed, troops wearing black rubber gas masks arrived on the scene and controlled the "mob" with tear gas.

And so it has come to this

In Passing, Glass Coffins

ATLANTA (AP)—An Atlanta mortician has adopted the drive-in approach for busy persons who want to drive by and view a deceased friend.

Hirschel Thornton is building five windows in a row as an extension on his funeral home. Each window is six feet long and will contain a body in its coffin. The display will face a driveway at the side of the home located on a busy street.

"So many people want to come by and see the remains of a relative or friend," Thornton said, "but they just don't have the time. This way, they can drive by and just keep on going."

"The deceased will be lying in a lighted window, sort of tilted to the front so they can conveniently be seen," he added.

Where did he get the idea for the drive-in window?

"It's purely imagination," he said. "I dreamed it one night." Thornton said a surprising number of persons like to view a body in the late hours—midnight and 1 a.m.—for reasons of their own.

"Perhaps it's because they work late. But this habit keeps attendants at the funeral home answering the phone at all hours. And the drive-in window will eliminate these interruptions," he said.

U.S. Errors Laid to Glut Of Spy Data

WASHINGTON, July 9 (UPI) — A House subcommittee reported today that spies for the United States were collecting information so fast that their chiefs did not have time to read it. The backlog, the panel said, may have contributed to recent intelligence failures such as capture of the intelligence ship U.S.S. Pueblo off North Korea.

The Defense Appropriations subcommittee said unprocessed reports on Southeast Asia alone recently filled 517 linear feet of file drawer space at the headquarters of the Defense Intelligence Agency. The agency was created in 1961 five months after the failure of the Bay of Pigs invasion.

Committee members, in published testimony on D.I.A. operations, said the undigested information might have contributed to the Pueblo seizure, the Israeli attack on the Liberty, another intelligence ship, and the lack of advance information about the Communist Tet offensive in Vietnam.

"Within D.I.A. it takes an average of eight workdays from the time of receipt for a document to reach the analysts," the subcommittee reported.

"One could only conclude that the management of your intelligence assets is in a state of complete disarray," Representative Jamie L. Whitten, Democrat of Mississippi, told D.I.A. officials.

The system will collapse under its own weight. Our job is to give it a few kicks and stay high.

10

EGO TRIPPING

LOVE & DOING YOUR THING

"I saw a man making love to his wife in Chicago . . ."
— Words to an old favorite

About a year and a half ago, while I was working at Liberty House, a girl came in to volunteer. We got to talking about civil rights, the South and so on. She asked me about drugs. I asked if she had ever taken LSD. When she responded that she hadn't, I threw her a white capsule. She juggled it the way you would a lighted firecracker. That night we made love and we've been doing it ever since. Three months later we got married in Central Park. It was a beautiful June day. Linn House, on STP, played the part of the Boo-Hoo priest. Marty was best man, Fouratt, flower boy, and lots of our friends came. We were dressed all in white with daisies in our hair. The *I Ching* was cast and the following message turned up:

CONFLICT.
YOU ARE SINCERE
AND ARE BEING OBSTRUCTED.
A CAUTIOUS HALT HALFWAY BRINGS GOOD
    FORTUNE.
GOING THROUGH TO THE END BRINGS MIS-
FORTUNE.
IT FURTHERS ONE TO SEE THE GREAT MAN.
IT DOES NOT FURTHER ONE TO CROSS THE
    GREAT WATER.

Conflict develops when one feels himself to be in the right and runs into opposition. If one is not convinced of being in the right, opposition leads to craftiness or high-handed encroachment but not to open conflict.

If a man is entangled in conflict, his only salvation lies in being so clear-headed and inwardly strong that he is always ready to come to terms by meeting the opposition halfway. To carry on the conflict to the bitter end has evil effects even when one is in the right, because the enmity is then perpetuated. It is important to see the great man, that is, an impartial man whose authority is great enough to terminate the conflict amicably or assure a just decision. In times of strife, crossing the great water is to be avoided, that is, dangerous enterprises are not to be begun, because in order to be successful they require concerted unity of forces. Conflict within weakens the power to conquer danger without.

We live without conflict in a small apartment that we designed ourselves in the exact center of the busiest street (Saint Marx Place) on the Lower East Side. We spend most of our time in a bed we built seven feet off the floor. There are no railings on the bed. Our love is strong enough to keep us suspended even if the bed collapsed.

Love is doing what you want to do, it's not all that give-and-take horseshit we were taught to believe. Anita has a Masters in psychology; once she entered Dorian Grey into a mental hospital. Now she spends most of her time stringing beads. I fell in love with her when she told me she didn't want to do anything. She is a true drop-out, a drop-out that could have made it, and made it big in the other world.

Thursday afternoon in Chicago, Ron (who had driven me around most of the time in Chicago, guarding me like a mother hen — even saving my life one night when he found his landlord at the front door of our apartment with a pistol), Anita and I walked along Michigan Avenue in front of the Conrad Hitler Hotel. I said I was going to march to the Amphitheater. Anita, who would rather sleep than march, said she was going back to the apartment. We kissed and parted. Ron came with me, reluctantly though, he didn't want to go on the march. He criticized me for not having more regard for Anita's feelings. "Ron," I said, "the reason you and I are just friends, and Anita and I are in love, is that Anita and I both do what we

want." I think he finally understood because he left me and I
didn't see him again that day.*

POOL HUSTLING & BRAGGING

I've done a lot of things in my time, but it's funny, I always
used to get to be second best. That is, I'd keep challenging
people better than me until I met someone I knew I couldn't
beat, then I'd switch to something else. The switching helped
me learn an awful lot about a lot of things.

At eleven I could deal off the bottom of the deck in poker;
by thirteen I didn't have to, I was so good. I have beaten
everyone I've played in gin rummy. For a few years I used to
play the horses every day and I still occasionally glance at the
Morning Telegraph, one of the best papers in America. I've
been in six-day crap games, where you develop a certain pac-
ing that helps in situations like Chicago. I lost in Las Vegas,
though. Gambling for high stakes, free and loose, taught me
that money is only a prop, only a stake in the game. I guess
all Diggers are gamblers.

At fifteen I learned how to steal cars. I have always been
good at shop-lifting. At seventeen I got thrown out of high
school for hitting a teacher and got stabbed in the leg in a
gang fight. It was sort of weird, being a nice Jewish boy and

---

* This is the only section of the book I am dissatisfied with. I am
tempted to discard it, but I won't. Love is the one thing easiest to do
and the most difficult to talk about. Few readers can understand the
difficulties of being married to a revolutionist. Anita is a rare one
indeed.

all. Then I went to prep school and later Brandeis and Berkeley, where I think I got a Masters in psychology — at least I
got the credits to become a state psychologist in Massachusetts.
I did testing and research in a mental hospital for two years.
I experienced a bum marriage (help stamp out first marriages)
which produced two beautiful kids. I am a natural cook, which
means I don't use a measuring cup. I have been a:

> drug salesman
> ghetto organizer
> campaign coordinator (peace campaign of Stuart Hughes
>   and Thomas Adams, both in Massachusetts)
> SNCC field worker
> movie theater manager
> grinder in an airplane factory
> camp counselor
> cook

I came to New York to start Liberty House in the West Village, which I designed, hustled the bread for, painted, and got
sore fingers banging in the nails. I worked there seven days a
week for $40.

I was always better at games than working. I was a Duncan
Yo-Yo champion (remember the Filipino that came around with
all the fancy tricks. He would carve initials in your yo-yo if you
were good). My parents' house is cluttered with trophies from
bowling, tennis, ping-pong, and autocar racing. I was captain
of the tennis team in college, member of the wrestling team,
and a member of a modern dance class. I played halfback on
the junior varsity football team at Worcester Academy (the
team played all the high schools around) and at 135 pounds
that was an accomplishment. I broke my arm in one game. I
did the Mississippi and Georgia tour of duty. I can roller skate
fantastically as well as dance and fuck like no one I've ever
met. I am good at golf, chess, bridge, basketball, and baseball.
I have burned my draft card. I can pitch very good softball and
play third base well. Last year in Newark I played tackle football with some black guys without any equipment and knew I

was a hot shit. I can do all sorts of somersaults and acrobatic things, know party tricks galore and can hypnotize almost anyone. I have run with the bulls in Pamplona. I wear out six pairs of heels on my boots each year. I can ride a motorcycle. I never sit still and contrary to rumor don't use speed. I run on piss and vinegar. This is my form of meditation. I studied French for about seven years, including three weeks at the Institut d'Etudion Français, and I can speak practically none at all. I took music lessons on a variety of instruments each for about a week and can't play a one. The Group Image used to let me get up on stage and sing with Sheila Shelby, but now they want to make money. (The Fugs are more than a musical group, they are a way of life that is OK Tapioca.) The Doors are my favorite rock group. They are the only group I can sit and listen to; the rest require dancing. I get bored at concerts and plays and only movies keep me totally absorbed. Some movies like *Viking Queen, Rosemary's Baby, 2001, The Professionals, Wild in the Streets, Battle of Algiers* I find fantastically compelling. I walked out of *La Chinoise* and in general find American movies better than foreign ones except for Fellini. I have been disappointed with Truffaut and Bergman lately. I love going to movies at the St. Marks Theater, where you can see two for seventy cents and yell, hiss, and get stoned on inhaling, there are so many people turning on. Bob Dylan and the Beatles are so great I hesitate to even mention them. I don't care for Joan Baez. One of my favorite groups is called the Lower East Side. They are led by Dave Peel and sing in the streets for FREE. I have what psychologists call eidetic imagery and an I.Q. of 78, resulting from over seventy LSD trips. I love Marvel comics and Moxie is my favorite drink, but unfortunately you can get it only in Massachusetts.

That ain't half of it, but if I wanted to be known for anything I guess it would be for my ability to hustle pool. Pool-hustling is a fine and delicate art. I'm one of the best there is. That doesn't mean I'm necessarily one of the best pool players. There are thousands of better players than me. A pool-hustler is a guy who plays only people he can beat. I was very young when I began hanging around pool halls. I used to bowl a lot and I became fascinated by the poolhall scene in the back of most bowling alleys: the old Buddhas sitting around the tables, following each shot, rarely making a sound; the ritualistic dances the players made; the pool-talk language; the battlefield of green felt, sixteen cannon balls of multicolored ivory, and rifle butts of long straight cue sticks. I was especially impressed, of course, by super hustlers who carried their own pool sticks. In a religious ceremony that would rival the Eucharist they would unpack and screw together the various parts of their cue sticks, powder their hands, spit in the corner, and be ready. The act of being "ready" in a pool game is the act of being ready in the world. After a year of solid practice, I finally earned the privilege of having a cue stick with my name on it placed in a special rack on the wall. For the next few years I practiced hustling. You know, walking into a pool hall, running a few racks fairly well, not as good as you really are. For the art of pool-hustling is to be only good enough to win. When some guy comes up and says, "Hey kid, how about some nine-ball?" that's the point at which you have to know everything there is to know. Examine the way he walks, how he grabs the stick out of the rack. Estimate the cost of his shoes (a clue to how much money he has in his pocket). Should it be money up front or can he be trusted? Do you beat him straight out or lose the first game or two? How much time has he got? Can you learn anything from him even if he's better than you? (Play for low stakes.) Most importantly, can he beat you? It's the knack of answering that question that makes the difference between a good hustler and a fish. It's being a good pool-hustler that has kept me alive.

One night in Chicago Anita and I went into a pool hall. One of these fancy family billiard parlors with mostly lousy players and Muzak. I shot two racks without missing — rat — tat — tat, like a machine gunner bouncing around the table. I made fancy show-off shots like behind-the-backers and one where you roll the ball down the table and then slam it into the corner pocket with the cue ball. I didn't miss a trick. It was the best pool I had ever played in my entire life.

HOW TO WRITE
A BOOK OF GARBAGE

Parts of this book I had already written over the past year. I have tried to keep them in chronological order. I wanted to include parts written before Chicago, even though they are not as good, because I wanted to show a development and to emphasize the point that for me, and I know for many others, Chicago didn't begin on August 25th. There was a good deal of editing to do and, in addition, everything about the uses of the media, hustling, and Chicago had to be written. I called Joyce, my editor, on Friday, August 30th, and said I would have the book finished by Tuesday morning. That gave me three days, which would be all the time I needed. I write longhand in the tradition of Hemingway and Mailer, whom I admire. I have tried talking into a tape recorder or transcribing speeches but thought it was cheating. Anita types up each section and I rarely correct a word. It flows out like poetic garbage. It is written on the run. Even as I write, the middle finger on my right hand aching with pain, I am hustling lawyers and bail money for the Chicago Veterans, running back and forth to the FREE STORE, and listening to kids explore their problems in the kitchen. Nothing has changed. Life goes on as usual. The book is just another part of life. A kid tells a story, a trigger flashes in my head, and in goes another page of garbage.

I hope there are a lot of misspellings in the book that get by fussbudget editors and proofreaders. Misspellings get the reader involved. I try to use words as images. I suggest people get into. reading Benjamin Whorf. Whorf was a very interesting guy. An insurance investigator in Hartford, Connecticut, he made a lasting contribution to the psychology of communication. He was on assignment investigating explosions in warehouses. It seemed that truck drivers with lighted cigars were walking into "empty" warehouses that contained gases and setting off explosions. BOOM! Whorf started contemplating the word "empty" and realized that we associate empty with harmless. He developed a theory called the "Whorf Hypothesis," which states that "language shapes our environment." I forget the name of his book, but it is worth looking up.

I have only glanced at the contract, have no lawyer and no agent. I still believe in the power of a handshake. I've kept my name off the book as well as off *Fuck the System* for a variety of reasons. One is that I would like people to use the books as props to help them hustle. That is, say they wrote them. I've done that when I want a free meal or to meet someone. Maybe I left it off because I'm on the biggest ego trip of them all. Maybe I'm for real?

The profits of the book that are my share will be taken out in free books and distributed by the FREE STORE for nothing at 14 Cooper Square, New York City. If you paid money for the book you got screwed. We want to take the Pig on tour with a rock-light, rabble-rousing, sock-it-to-Humphrey caravan. We want to tour Europe and end up at the inauguraation next January. We are currently entering a $100,000,000 lawsuit against Mayor Daley and the City of Chicago, and Bill Kunstler, the best Movement lawyer, thinks we have a chance to win. If we did I would like us to rent the International Amphitheater and have a huge rally for the Pig, inviting all the veterans back. I would also like to see us offer $10,000 to every cop in Chicago who agreed to quit the police force. That would leave about five thousand bucks or so, just about enough to set Jim Morrison up in an underground laboratory here in New York so he could continue producing that fantastic Honey. I have never had such powerful dope. He was the real hero of the Battle of Chicago.

I GET BY WITH
A LITTLE HELP FROM MY FRIENDS

Thanks to:
MARTY — SUSAN — JASON — SARAH — GINSBERG —
PAUL — ED — TULI — JERRY — NANCY — KEITH — STU
— PETER RABBIT — EMMETT — PETER — CHÉ — DYLAN
—SANDI—JOHN—CATHY—MORNING DOVE—HO-CHI-
MINH — JOHN AND FLORENCE — JACK AND PHYLLIS —
SHEILA — AMI — ANDREW — DON — GARY — ELLEN —
DANNY — ALLAN — LENNOX — MARSHALL — RAY —
PHIL — CAROL — TOBY — COLLEEN — JULIUS — **ANITA**
— FRED — ROBIN — SHARON — THE RESISTANCE —
DICK DALEY — RUNNING WATER — FRANKIE SPADE —
CAPTAIN FINK — THE MOTHERFUCKERS — TOM AND
RENNIE — LBJ — JIM MORRISON AND HIS HONEY —
ABE MASLOW — PETER AND KATE — MANNY — IRA —
MARIO — MARTY'S MOTHER — ERNIE KOVACS — JIM
AND PAT — BOB AND BRIGIT — JACQUES — SAUL —
LINN — ARTAUD — BILLY — TOM — GREG — HASKELL
— THE BLACKSTONE RANGERS — FREE CITY SAN
FRANCISCO (THE CHURCH OF MY CHOICE) — LEAH AND
ALAN — CHINO — RAP — PAULA — JOYCE — LENNY
BRUCE — THE FREEDOM SCHOOL KIDS FROM McCOMB,
MISSISSIPPI — FATHER GILGUN — LEARY — SOUTHEY
— BRAD — MARC — HARVEY — THE HEAD HUNTERS
MOTORCYCLE CLUB — ABE — HERBIE — RON — THE
BEATLES — HUMP — GEORGE METESKY — MARAT —
THE BASKINS — MICKEY — JIM PIERSALL — CHAIRMAN
MAO — STEVE — VITO — CARLOS — MALCOLM X —
DIANA — BUCKY — JUDY — IRON MIKE — STAUGHTON

LYND — JUDGE LYNCH — PIG LYNSKY — JOHN WALRUS
— AL — HUGH — KESEY — FRANKIE ABBOTT — OFFICER
HENLEY AND HIS GOLD BULLET — THE DIGGERS —
MAX — W. C. FIELDS — PIG — THE OTHER JIM MORRI-
SON — McLUHAN — STOKELY — CHARLIE — MITCH —
AARON — GLORIA — ERIC AND HIS MEGAPHONE —
THE BLACK PANTHERS — HAL — MARCUSE — SANDY
AND EVENING FIRE — BARRY — JIMMY BRESLIN —
LARRY MERCHANT — TOM AND LESLIE — DAVE —
MOTORCYCLE RICHIE — ARTI — COUSIN CLYDE — LEE
— ABBIE — WREN — THE LOWER EAST SIDE SINGERS
— RANDY — VALERIE AND ANDY — MENDY — LNS —
BONNIE AND CLYDE — TODAY — NORMAN MAILER —
JESUS — HOME JUICE — MC5 — COUNTRY JOE —
SUPER JOEL — MARVIN AND BARBARA — JESSE MOR-
RIS — DORIS — FANNIE LOU HAMER — HUEY — PHIL —
DIANNE — ELDRIDGE — ANNE — BUNNY — TRUCIA —
WOLF — TOKYO ROSE — YOSSARIAN — SIDDHARTHA
— MAO — SERGEANT SUNSHINE — THE LISTENERS OF
WBAI-FM's RADIO UNNAMEABLE — J. EDGAR FREAKO
— THE GROUCHY WAITERS FROM B & H LUNCHEON-
ETTE — RUDI — CLEVE — WORTH — GENERAL GIAP —
ALBERT PARKER — IVANHOE — SCHWERNER, GOOD-
MAN & CHANEY — AND TO DON McNEILL, WHO DIDN'T
LIVE TO MAKE IT TO CHICAGO, AND DEAN JOHNSON,
WHO GAVE HIS LIFE THERE, AND FINALLY TO ESTHER
FROM SCHACHTS' ON SECOND AVENUE, WHO GAVE ME
SOME FREE CHEESE YESTERDAY WHEN THE BOSS
WASN'T LOOKING, **IT SURE IS A HELL OF A CON-
SPIRACY!**

11

EPILOGUE

Tuesday, September 17, 1968, was one hell of a day. I returned to Chicago with my attorney, Jerry Lefcourt, to stand trial for the infamous four-letter WORD on my forehead. I wanted to clear this matter up because I expected trouble at Customs when I attempted to leave to go to Prague. As we stepped off the airplane at O'Hare Airport, we were met by six of Chicago's finest. I was immediately handcuffed and arrested on a charge of jumping bail even though it was obvious to everyone I had only come back to Chicago to appear in court that afternoon. I was questioned in a special room in the airport and when asked to empty my pockets, I produced a pen knife I had purchased the day before in New York. It is a knife that is legal in every state of the union. The cops couldn't figure out how to open it so dubbed it a switchblade. After I was taken to court to stand trial for the WORD and to be arraigned on bail-jumping charges (these charges were dropped), I was again arrested by the Chicago police for carrying a concealed weapon. When bail was produced on this charge, I was then arrested by the FBI and charged with "crimes aboard an aircraft." The FBI is the only agency in the country that arrests you and makes it seem like they are doing you a favor. The dialogue went something like this:

FBI: You are now being placed under arrest for crimes aboard an aircraft.

ME: Are you kidding? All I did was goose the stewardess, what crimes?

FBI: Our instructions are to tell you only that. We must warn you that anything you say may be used against you. We'll just settle this before the U.S. Commissioner, it won't take long. We are sorry to inconvenience you this way.

ME: Can I call my wife and tell her I'll be home late from work?

FBI: Yes, we think that is certainly a most reasonable request.

In the car, driving to the Federal Building, they asked if I used any aliases. I gave them enough for three sheets of paper.

They recorded them all diligently, including Casey Stengal, George Metesky, Spiro Agnew, and Muriel Humphrey. Lo and behold, the Commissioner wasn't home and it was into the jail for the night. Chicago city jails, by the way, have the worst food of any jails I have ever been in. That morning I appeared before a U.S. Commissioner who looked like the guy who played the telephone booth in *The President's Analyst*. The "crimes aboard an aircraft" revolved around the mysterious pen knife and the judge was very serious. Here is some of the dialogue:

COMMISSIONER: When you came to Chicago you said you were unemployed?

ME: Well, thanks to the Chicago police, I've become a very successful writer. I just finished a book about Chicago, a children's book, and I'm working on a movie. I made $10,000 this week, but I plan to burn it all.

COMMISSIONER: Have you ever been arrested?

ME: I've been arrested over twenty times, but I've never been convicted. There are a lot of cops breaking the law in this country.

COMMISSIONER: Have you ever jumped bail?

ME: Only once, in Mississippi, but it was under unusual circumstances.

COMMISSIONER: What were they?

ME: The Ku Klux Klan was organizing a lynching party and my attorney thought it wise if I blew town.

COMMISSIONER: Does the District Attorney demand bail?

D.A.: The People ask $1500 bail, your honor.

COMMISSIONER: I think I'll make that $2500 and you are confined to Chicago and the Federal District of Manhattan.

ME: Can I go to Prague?

COMMISSIONER: No.

ME: Well, if you think the U.S. Government can handle the Czechoslovakian mess better than the Yippies, you can have that one. Can I go to Massachusetts to visit my mother?

COMMISSIONER: No.

ME: Can I go above 14th Street?

COMMISSIONER: Yes, but you cannot leave Manhattan except to return to Chicago.

ME: I want you to know that I accuse you and the Federal Government of committing an unjust act of revenge.

I turned around and walked out of the courtroom. Much to my surprise, the Commissioner did nothing.

It had been some day. I had been fingerprinted no less than seventeen times and spent most of the time in various sets of handcuffs. As I was sitting in the airplane waiting to fly back to New York, the pilot made an announcement that the flight would be delayed fifteen minutes. Five men entered the airplane. Four, I recognized as members of the Chicago Intelligence Division that had been following me throughout the Convention, the other identified himself as a U.S. Marshal. He handed me a piece of paper which began, "Greetings: You are hereby commanded to appear before the House Un-American Activities Committee. . ." It was like receiving a high school diploma.

The time since Chicago has been filled with persistent government harassment. On three occasions a phony Brink's truck has stopped outside our FREE STORE on the Lower East Side, a panel opens up and a camera begins taking photographs. I have been visited no less than five times by FBI agents, twice by Justice Department officials and once by the Internal Revenue Service.

On Tuesday, October 2, 1968, we appeared before HUAC. Jerry wore a one-man, world-conspiracy, guerrilla costume complete with toy M-16 and live ammunition. I went as an Indian with feathers, hunting knife, and a bullwhip. I also carried an electric yoyo and dazzled the Committee with tricks like, "Around-the-Capitalist-World," "Split-the-Southern-Cracker," and "Burning-Down-the-Town." On the first day, the hearing was very dull. HUAC missed Joe Pool and at one point I suggested we have five minutes of silence in his memory. When the Committee refused, I accused them of being "soft on Communism." I persisted in asking permission to go to the bathroom and pointing out to the Committee the different people in the room who were carrying guns (all Capitol guards, of course, but you never can tell, some sneaky Yippie might have rented a cop suit). Jerry walked around waving his gun and rattling his bells, his girlfriend Nancy was dressed as a Halloween witch and passed out incense. The Committee dragged on with boring testimony trying to link us to Communists (many of whom were active before we were born), and even at one point to Lee Harvey Oswald. The acting chairman of the Committee made repeated warnings against "emotional outbursts." By about three o'clock, I was so bored I couldn't take it any longer. I asked permission to make an emotional outburst. They said not in the room, so I retired to the hall and shouted, "You're full of shit" so loud it shook the Capitol Building. When the cops tried to jump me, I told them the Committee requested I do it in the hall. They let me go. Thirty minutes later, the lawyers who had been raising objections throughout the day stood in protest with their clients. They were hustled out by the cops and that ended Act I.

Wednesday, we broke for Yom Kippur or the World Series, and the Committee carried on in closed session. They heard all about the Yippie plans to assassinate Mayor Daley and blow up a baseball diamond in Lincoln Park. A secret "deal" was revealed that showed we had arranged with the Headhunter Motorcycle Club to provide them with girls and dope if they would furnish us ammunition. At one point, we were accused of going to Chicago "to perform magic."

Thursday, I appeared in a commercially made shirt that has red and white stripes and stars on a blue background. Capitol police arrested me for mutilating the flag and proceeded to rip the shirt off my back. Anita screamed and was arrested for felonious assault on a policeman. Anita's charges were later dropped. I had to spend the night in jail (the judge originally set bail at $3000, which kind of shocked everyone) and then I was detained an extra five hours by U.S. Marshals illegally. Of course, the terms "legal" and "illegal" are phrases lawyers throw back and forth and have nothing to do with the reality of what's happening in the judicial system in this country. The law I was arrested under would make everyone who dresses in an Uncle Sam costume and most drum majorettes criminals. The other night, I watched Phyllis Diller perform on national television in a miniskirt that looked more like an American Flag than the shirt I wore.

The hearings were adjourned to Thursday and we were ordered to return December 2, 1968 to begin our testimony. I plan to reveal everything. But I must warn the Committee that there will be a continuing language barrier. I requested permission to bring an interpreter to the October hearings, but permission was denied. I brought her anyway, but it was still difficult to understand them. They spoke of Marx and I thought they meant Groucho. My interpreter said, "No, they mean Karl Marx." They spoke of Lenin and I thought they meant John Lennon of the Beatles. My interpreter said, "No, they mean the guy without a first name." It was all getting very confusing, but what's to be expected when CHROMOSOME DAMAGE meets the DINOSAURS. One thing I will state, however, before I even testify is that "I am not now nor have I ever been a member of the House Un-American Activities Committee."

12

THIS PART IS
ABSOLUTELY FREE

REVIEW OF *FUCK THE SYSTEM*

Fuck the System is the most interesting book I've read this year. It also happens to be the only one. That's probably because most books deal with issues and issues are not relevant to my revolution. What we need is information that helps us solve problems. Where do I get food when I'm hungry? How can I sneak into the movies? What do I do when I get busted? How do I spot the clap? Where can I get an abortion? How can I make a Molotov Cocktail? The politics of the book speaks for itself. No long essay on the evils of corporate liberalism, capitalism is never mentioned, yet the book implies a system in which private ownership is abolished. It hints at something beyond communism. Communism is the correct alternative to capitalism if one finds oneself in the midst of an industrial revolution. It makes sense to join the workers together, establish a concept of national trade unionism, and fight the tyrannical bosses if the economics of the system fit. Those radicals that dream of taking to the streets and a week later having a national general strike à la France are stoned out of their minds. The truth of the matter is that most workers in America have a good deal materialistically. Secondly, the struggle between the working class and the bosses in traditional Marxist economy theory is built on a premise of security. With the introduction of cybernation into industry we have a glimpse of economic theory built on a premise of abundance. The details of such an economic theory remain to be worked out but the means of reaching a Free society are not that difficult (at least postulating them is not that difficult). A good many people will have to change their ideas on competition vs. cooperation, work vs. play, postponement of pleasure vs. instant gratification. It is also obvious that a lot of fat cats living high off the hog are going to have to get their asses kicked. But above all this, more people have to begin to live the revolution and to live it now. George Metesky does just that.

Seven years ago George was just a lonely guy working for Con Edison. He had worked 15 years in the accounting department doing stamp and file work 9 to 5, five days a week. One day he got fed up and started returning customers' checks with a small note saying they had already paid the bill. Con Edison found out about it, fired George and soon was responsible for George taking revenge on the property system. For six months George left three-inch pipe-and-gunpowder bombs in various buildings around New York. Most of them never really went off but the whole city was scared shitless every time meek Georgie went into his back room laboratory and came out as "The Mad Bomber." One day George got tired and a little careless so the fuzz grabbed him. Released from jail a few years ago, George spends most of his time publishing poems and booklets such as *Fuck the System*, attacking the property fetish of America. He also does a little counterfeiting on the side to support himself and his friends in the style to which they are accustomed. His son, Jim, lives on the Lower East Side and divides his time between banging nails in police car tires, passing out free LSD, and burning money at the Stock Exchange.

The booklet raises some basic questions: "If we have so much extra shit lying around how come we have ten million poor people in the country?" I think it is that contradiction that keeps many of us in the streets picketing or throwing Molotov Cocktails or whatever else is handy. Here we have, for example, the Cuban Revolution only eleven years old and they already have free phones, free bus rides, 60 percent of the housing free, free medical service, and free food on all crops of which there is an abundance. On the Isle of Pines in Cuba, eighty thousand young people are busy working out the dynamics of a money-free society in an experimental situation supported by the government. Fidel states candidly that the goal of the Cuban Revolution is the abolition of money. My God, our revolution is close to two hundred years old and you have to pay ten cents to take a shit in the train station while we spend thirty billion in Vietnam, to say nothing of those ten million poor.

A final basic question is: "What would happen if large numbers of people really do decide to fuck the system?" The little book is a sort of Bible and it's not unusual to hear young smiling barefoot kids on the Lower East Side saying they live by the book. What would happen if large numbers of people in the country started getting together, forming communities, hustling free fish on Fulton Street, and passing out brass washers to use in the laundromats and phones? What if people living in slums started moving into abandoned buildings and refusing to move even to the point of defending them with guns? What if this movement grew and busy salesmen sweating under the collar on a hot summer day decided to say fuck the system and headed for welfare? What if secretaries got tired of typing memos to the boss's girlfriend in triplicate and took to panhandling in the streets? What if when they called a war, no one went? What if people who wanted to get educated just went to a college classroom and sat-in without paying and without caring about a degree? Well, you know what? We'd have ourselves one hell of a revolution, that's what. "Who would do the work?" Fuck it. There's always some schmuck like Spiro Agnew lying around. Let him pick up the garbage if he's worried about the smell. We'll build a special zoo for people like that and every weekend we'll take the kiddies over to Queens to watch them work. Needless to say, the zoo will be free and if history deems it otherwise and you have to pay to get in, ol' George Metesky will come around and put out another booklet on how to sneak into zoos.

POLICE PATR

*Now What
Do You Want?*

Fuck the System

POLICE DEPT.
NINTH PCT.

**Take what you want
Take what you need
There is plenty to go around
Everything is free.**

George Metesky

Free

New York

YIPPIEEEEEEEEEEEEEEEEEEEEEEEEEEEEEEEEEEEEEEEEEEEEEEEEEEEEEEEEEEEE

TABLE OF CONTENTS

3

FREE VEGETABLES — Hunt's Point Market, Hunt's Point Avenue and 138th Street. Have to go by car or truck between 6-9 A.M. but well worth it. You can get enough vegetables to last your commune a week. Lettuce, squash, carrots, canteloupe, grapefruit, melons, even artichokes and mushrooms. Just tell them you want to feed some people free and it's yours, all crated and everything. Hunt's Point is the free people's heaven.

FREE MEAT AND POULTRY — The closest slaughterhouse area is in the far West Village, west of Hudson Street and south of 14th Street. Get a letter from Rev. Allen of St. Mark's on the Bowerie, Second Avenue and 10th Street, saying you need some meat for a church sponsored meal. If you want to be really professional, dress as a priest and go over and ask. Bring a car or truck. A freezer unit will save a good deal of running around. Don't give up on this one. Turning a guy onto the free idea will net you a week's supply of top quality meat. There is some law that if the meat touches the ground or floor they have to give it away. So if you know how to trip a meat truck, by all means . . .

FREE FRESH FISH — The Fish Market is located on Fulton Street and South Street under the East River Drive overpass. You have to get there between 6 - 9 A.M. but it is well worth it. The fishermen always have hundreds of pounds of fish that they have to throw away if they don't sell. Mackerel, halibut, cod, catfish, and more. You can have as much as you can cart away.

FREE BREAD AND ROLLS — Rapaports on Second Avenue between 5th and 6th Streets will give you all the free bread and rolls you can carry. You have to get there by 7:00 A.M. in order to get the stuff. It's a day old, but still very good. If you want them absolutely fresh, put them in an oven to which you have added a pan of water (to avoid drying them out), and warm them for a few minutes. Most bakeries will give you day old stuff if you give them a half way decent sob story.

★ ★ ★

A&P stores clean their vegetable bins every day at 9:00 A.M. They always throw out cartons of very good vegetables. Tell them you want to feed your rabbits. Also recommended is picking up food in a supermarket and eating it before you leave the store. This method is a lot safer than the customary shoplifting. In order to be prosecuted for shoplifting you have to leave the store with the goods. If you have eaten it, there is no evidence to be used against you.

FREE COOKING LESSONS — (Plus you get to eat the meal) are sponsored by the New York Department of Markets, 137 Centre Street. Thursday mornings. Call CA 6-5653 for more information.

Check the Yellow Pages for Catering Services. You can visit them on a Saturday, Sunday afternoon or Monday morning. They always have stuff left over. Invest 10c in one of the Jewish Dailies and check out the addresses of the local synagogues and their schedule of bar mitzvahs, weddings, and testimonial dinners. Show up at the back of the place about three hours after it is scheduled to start. There is always left-over food. Tell them you're a college student and want to bring some back for your fraternity brothers. Jews dig the college bullshit. If you want the food served to you out front you naturally have to disguise yourself to look straight. Remarks such as "I'm Marvin's brother" or — learning the bride's name from the paper — "Gee, Dorothy looks marvelous" are great. Lines like "Betty doesn't look pregnant" are frowned upon.

★ ★ ★

Large East Side bars are fantastically easy touches. The best time is 5:00 P.M. Take a half empty glass of booze from an empty table and use it as a prop. Just walk around sampling the hors d'oeuvres. Once you find your favorite, stick to it. You can soon become a regular. They won't mind your loading up on free food because they consider you one of the crowd. Little do they realize that you are a super freeloader. All Longchamps are good. Max's Kansas City at Park Avenue South and 16th Street

5

doesn't even mind it if you freeload when you are hungry and an advantage here is that you can wear any kind of clothes. Max features fried chicken wings, swedish meatballs and ravioli.

THE INTERNATIONAL SOCIETY FOR KRISHNA CONSCIOUSNESS is located at 26 Second Avenue. Every morning at 7:00 A.M. a delicious cereal breakfast is served free along with chanting and dancing. Also 12 Noon more food and chanting and on Monday, Wednesday and Friday at 7:00 P.M. again food and chanting. Then it's all day Sunday in Central Park Sheepmeadow (generally) for still more chanting (sans food). Hari Krishna is the freest high going if you can get into it and dig cereal and, of course, more chanting.

FREE TEA AND COOKIES — In a very nice setting at the Tea Center, 16 East 56th Street. 10 - 11 A.M. and 2 - 4 P.M. Monday to Friday.

THE CATHOLIC WORKER — 181 Chrystie Street, will feed you any time but you have to pray as you do in the various Salvation Army stations. Heavy wino scenes. The heaviest wino scene is the **Men's Temporary Shelter** on 8 East 3rd Street. You can get free room and / or meals here if you are over 21 but it's worse than jail or Bellevue. It is a definite last resort only.

The freest meal of all is Tuesdays at 5:00 P.M. inside or in front of St. Mark's Church on the Bowerie, Second Avenue at 10th Street. A few yippie-diggers serve up a meal ranging from Lion Meat to Guppy Chowder to Canteloupe Salad. They are currently looking for a free truck to help them collect the food and free souls dedicated to extending the free food concept. The Motherfuckers also dish out free food on St. Mark's Place from time to time.

If you are really looking for class, pick up a copy of the **New York Times** and check the box in the back pages designating ocean cruises. On every departure there is a bon voyage party. Just walk on a few hours before sailing time and start swinging. Champagne, caviar, lobster salad, all as free as the open sea. If you get stoned enough and miss getting off you can also wiggle a free boat ride although you get sent back as soon as you hit the other side — but it's a free ocean cruise, even if it's in the brig.

You can get free food in varying quantities by going to the factories. Many also offer a free tour. However, the plants are generally located outside of Manhattan. If you can get a car, try a trip to Long Island City. There you will find the Gordon Baking Company at 42-25 21st Street, Pepsi-Cola at 4602 Fifth Avenue, Borden Company at 35-10 Steinway Street and Dannon Yogurt at 22-11 38th Avenue. All four places give out free samples and if you write or call in advance and say it is for a block party or church affair, they will give you a few cases.

FREE BOOZE — Jacob Ruppert Brewery at 1639 Third Avenue near 91st Street will give you a tour at 10:30 A.M. and 2:30 P.M. complete with free booze in their tap room.

★ ★ ★

The Sun is free. Hair is freee. Naked bodies are free. Smiles are free. Rain is free. Unfortunately there is no free air in New York. Con Edison's phone number is 679-6700.

WELFARE — If you live in lower Manhattan the welfare center for you is located on 11 West 13th Street, 989-1210. There is, of course, red tape involved and they don't dig longhairs. Be prepared to tell a good story as to why you cannot work, however your looks (which they cannot make you change) might be good enough reason. This is

7

one place where sloppy clothes pay off. You have to be over 18 to get help. A caseworker will be assigned to you. Some will actually dig the whole scene and won't give you a hard time, others can be a real bitch. Getting on welfare can get you free rent, phone, utilities, and about $20.00 a week to live on. There are also various food stamp and medical programs you become eligible for. If you can stomach hassle, welfare is a must. The main office number is DI 4-8700 if you do not live in lower Manhattan.

FREE CLOTHES — Try ESSO, 341 East 10th Street or Tompkins Square Community Center on Avenue B and 9th Street. Also the streets are excellent places to pick up good clothes (see section on free furniture for best times to go hunting).

FREE LAWYERS — **Legal Aid Society,** 100 Centre Street, BE 3-0250 (criminal matters) and the **New York University Law Center Office,** 249 Sullivan Street, GR 3-1896 (civil matters). Also for specialized cases and information you can call the **National Lawyers Guild,** 5 Beekman Street, 227-1078 or the **New York Civil Liberties Union,** 156 Fifth Avenue, WA 9-6076. For the best help on the Lower East Side use **Mobilization for Youth Legal Services,** 320 East 3rd Street between Avenues C and D, OR 7-0400, ask for legal services. Open Tuesday to Friday, 9 A.M. to 6 P.M.. and until 8 P.M. on Mondays. Some of the best lawyers in the city available here.

FREE FLOWERS — At about 9:30 A.M. each day you can bum free flowers in the Flower District on Sixth Avenue between 22nd and 23rd Streets. Once in a while you can find a potted tree that's been thrown out because it's slightly damaged.

8

FREE FURNITURE — By far the best place to get free furniture is on the street. Once a week in every district the sanitation department makes bulk pick-ups. The night before residents put out all kinds of stuff on the street. For the best selection try the West Village on Monday nights and the east Seventies on Tuesday nights. On Wednesday night there are fantastic pick-ups on 35th Street in back of Macy's. Move quickly though, the guards get pissed off easily; the truckers couldn't care less. This street method can furnish your whole pad. Beds, desks, bureaus, lamps, bookcases, chairs, and tables. It's all a matter of transportation. If you don't have access to a car or truck it is almost worth it to rent a station wagon on a weekday and make pick-ups. Alexander's Rent-a-Car is about the cheapest for in-city use. $5.95 and 10c a mile for a regular car. A station wagon is slightly more. Call AG 9-2200 for the branch near you.

Also consider demolition and construction sites as a good source for building materials to construct furniture. The large wooden cable spools make great tables. Cinderblocks, bricks and boards for bookcases. Doors for tables. Nail kegs for stools and chairs.

FREE BUS RIDES — Get on with a large denomination bill just as the bus is leaving.

FREE SUBWAY RIDES — Get a dark green card and flash it quickly as you go through the exit gate. Always test the swing bars in the turnstile before you put in the token. Someone during the day was sure to drop an extra token in and a free turn is just waiting for the first one to take advantage of it. By far the most creative method is the use of German fennigs, Danish ore or Mozambique 10 centavos pieces. These fit most turnstiles except the newest (carry a real token to use in case the freebee doesn't work). These foreign coins come four or five to a penny. Large amounts must be purchased outside New York City. Most dealers will not sell you large amounts since the

Transit Authority has been pressuring them. Try telling dealers you want them to make jewelry. Another interesting coin is the 5 aurar from Iceland. This is the same size as a quarter and will work in most vending machines. They sell for three or four to the penny. There are other coins that also work. Buy a bag of assorted foreign coins from a coin dealer and do a little measuring. You are sure to find some that fit the bill. Speaking of fitting the bill, we have heard that dollar bills can be duplicated on any Xerox machine (fronts done separately from backs and pasted together) and used in vending machines that give change for a dollar. This method has not been field tested.

The best form of free transportation is hitch-hiking. This is so novel in New York that it often works. Crosstown on 8th Street is good.

FREE PHONE CALLS — A number 14 brass washer with a small piece of scotch tape over one side of the hole will work in old style phones (also parking meters, laundromat dryers, soda and other vending machines). The credit card bit works on long distance calls. Code letter for 1968 is J, then a phone number and then a three digit district number. A district number, as well as the phone number. can be made up by using any three numbers from about 051 to 735. Example: J-573-2100-421 or J-637-3400-302. The phone number should end in 00 since most large corporations have numbers that end that way. The people that you call often get weird phone calls from the company but not much else. There are also legitimate credit card numbers available. One recent number belonged to Steve McQueen. A phone bill of $50,000 was racked up in one month. McQueen, of course, was not held responsible.

FREE MONEY — Panhandling nets some people up to Twenty

dollars a day. The best places are Third Avenue in the fifties and the Theater District off Times Square. Both best in the evening on weekends. Uptown guys with dates are the best touch especially if they are just leaving some guilt movie like "Guess Who's Coming to Dinner?" The professional panhandlers don't waste their time on the Lower East Side except on weekends when the tourists come out.

Devise a street theatre act or troupe. It can be anything from a funny dance to a five piece band or a poetry reading. People give a lot more dough and the whole atmosphere sings a little. SMILE! Panhandle at the rectories and nunneries on the side of every Catholic Church. Contrary to rumor the brother and sister freeloaders in black live very well and will always share something with a fellow panhandler.

Also see previous sections on the use of foreign coins.

★ ★ ★

FREE BOOKS AND RECORDS — If you have an address you can get all kinds of books and records from clubs on introductory offers. Since the cards you mail back are not signed there is no legal way you can be held responsible although you get all sorts of threatening mail, which, by the way, also comes free.

You can always use the Public Libraries. The main branch is on Fifth Avenue and 42nd Street. There are 168 branches all over the city. Call OX 5-4200 for information and a schedule of free events.

POEMS are free. Are you a poem or are you a prose???

FREE GAS — If you have a car and need some gas late at night you can get a gallon and then some by emptying the hoses from the pumps into your tank. There is always a fair amount of surplus gas left when the pumps are shut off.

FREE LAND — Write to "Green Revolution" c/o School of Living, Freeland, Maryland, for their free newspaper with news about rural land available in the United States and the progress of various rural communities. The best available free land is in Canada. You can get a free listing by writing to the Department of Land and Forests, Parliament Building, Quebec City, Canada. Also write to the Geographical Branch, Department of Mines and Technical Surveys, Parliament Buildings, Quebec City, Canada. Lynn Burrows, c/o Communications Group, 2630 Point Grey Rd., Vancouver 8, British Columbia, Canada, will give you the best information on setting up a community in Canada.

If you really want to live for free, get some friends together and seize a building at Columbia University, 116th Street and Broadway. The cops come free, as do blue ribbon committees with funny long names.

FREE BUFFALO — In order to keep the herds at a controllable level the government will give you a real, live buffalo if you can guarantee shipping expenses and adequate grazing area. Write to the Office of Information, Department of the Interior, Washington, D.C.

MEDICAID — Medicaid Center, 330 West Street, 594-3050. Medicaid is a very good deal if you can qualify and can stand a little red tape. According to the new law you have to be under 21 or over 65 years of age and have a low income ($2900 or less if you are single) to qualify. It takes about a month to process your application, but if you get a card you are entitled to free hospital and dental services, private physicians, drugs and many other medical advantages.

AMBULANCE SERVICE — Call 440-1234. You get a cop free of charge with this service. There is no way to get an ambulance without a cop in New York.

EMERGENCY DOCTOR — TR 9-1000.
EMERGENCY DENTIST — YU 8-6110.
NEARBY HOSPITALS —
Gouverneur Clinic, 9 Gouverneur Slip, 227-3000.
St. Vincent Hospital, 7th Ave. and West 11th St., 620-1234.
Bellevue Hospital, First Avenue and 27th Street, 679-5487.
On the above medical services you have to pay but you can file the bill or send it to the National Digger Client Center in Washington, D.C. They will pay it for you.

THE WASHINGTON HEIGHTS HEALTH CENTER — 168th Street and Broadway, provides free chest X-rays as well as other services. You can get a free smallpox vaccination here at 10: A.M. weekdays if you're traveling abroad. Call WA 7-6300 for information.
See special section on clap in this booklet for information on VD treatment.

FREE DRUGS — In the area along Central Park West in the 70's and 80's are located many doctor's offices. Daily they throw out piles of drug samples. If you know what you're looking for, search this area.

FREE SECURITY — For this trick you need some money to begin with. Deposit it in a bank and return in a few weeks telling them you lost your bank book. They give you a card to fill out and sign and in a week you will receive another. Now, withdraw your money, leaving you with your original money and a bank book showing a balance. You can use this as identification, to prevent vagrancy busts traveling, as collateral for bail, or for opening a charge account at a store.

FREE BIRTH CONTROL INFORMATION AND DEVICES — **Clergy Consultation Abortion,** call 477-0034 and you will get a recorded announcement giving you the names of clergymen who you can call and get birth control information, including abortion contacts.

Parents Aid Society, 130 Main Street, Hempstead, Long Island, (516) 538-2626, provides by far the most complete birth control information. Pills are provided as well as diaphrams. Referrals are made to doctors willing to perform abortions despite their illegality because of medieval, menopausal politicians. Call them for an appointment before you go out there. They are about to establish an office on the Lower East Side.

FREE INFORMATION — Yippie: Youth International Party, 32 Union Square East, 982-5090.
ESSO — East Side Service Organization, 341 East 10th St., 533-5930.

DIAL-A-DEMONSTRATION — 924-6315 to find out about anti-war rallies and demonstrations.

DIAL-A-SATELLITE — TR 3-0404 to find out schedules of satellites.

NERVOUS can be dialed for the time.
WEATHER REPORT — WE 6-1212.
DIAL-A-PRAYER — CI 6-4200. God is a long - distance call.

If you want someone to talk you out of jumping out of a window call IN 2-3322.

★ ★ ★

If you have nothing to do for a few minutes, call the Pentagon (collect) and ask for Colonel John Masters of the Inter-Communication Center. Ask him how the war's going. (202) LI 5-6700.

★ ★ ★

If you want the latest news information you can call the wire services: **AP** is PL 7-1312 or **UPI** is MU 2-0400.

LIBERATION NEWS SERVICE — At 3064 Broadway and 121st Street will give you up to the minute coverage of movement news both national and local, as well as a more

14

accurate picture of what's going on. Call 865-1360. By the way, what is going on?

THE EAST VILLAGE OTHER — Office at 105 Second Avenue and 6th Street, 228-8640 might be able to answer some of your questions.

THE DAILY NEWS INFORMATION BUREAU — 220 East 42nd Street, MU 2-1234, will try to answer any question you put to them unless it's "Why do we need the Daily News?"

THE NEW YORK TIMES RESEARCH BUREAU — 229 West 43rd Street, LA 4-1000 will research news questions that pertain to the past three months if you believe there was a past three months.

FREE lessons in a variety of skills such as plumbing, electricity, jewelry making, construction and woodworking are provided by the Mechanics Institute, 20 West 44th Street. Call or write them well in advance for a schedule. You must sign up early for lessons as they try to maintain small courses. MU 7-4279.

Ron Rosen at 68 Thompson Street will give you free Karate lessons if he considers you in the movement.

FREE YOGA LESSONS — Yoga Institute, 50 East 81st Street, LE 5-0126. Call in advance for lecture schedule. You might be asked to do some voluntary kitchen yoga after the lessons.

FREE RENT — There are many abandoned buildings that are still habitable, especially if you know someone with electrical skills who, with a minimum of effort can supply you with free electricity. You can be busted for criminal trespassing but many people are getting away with it. If you are already in an apartment, eviction proceedings

15

in New York take about six months even if you don't pay rent.

You can sleep in the parks during the day. Day or night you can sleep on the roofs which are fairly safe and comfortable if you can find a shady spot. The tar gets very hot when the sun comes out. Make friends with someone in the building, then if the cops or landlord or other residents give you a problem you can say you are staying with someone in the building. Stay out of hallways, don't sleep on streets or stoops, or in the parks at night.

FREE BEACHES — Coney Island Beach (ES 2-1670) and Manhattan Beach on Oriental Boulevard (DE 2-6794) are two in Brooklyn that are free. Call for directions on how to get there. The Bronx offers Orchard Beach, call TT 5-1828 for information.

FREE COLLEGE — If you want to go to college free send away for the schedule of courses at the college of your choice. Pick your courses and walk into the designated classrooms. In some smaller classes this might be a problem but in large classes, of which there are hundreds in New York, there is no problem. If you need books for the course, write to the publisher telling him you are a lecturer at some school and are considering using the book in your course.

FREE THEATRE — **The Dramatic Worshop** — Studio # 808, Carnegie Hall Building, 881 Seventh Avenue at 56th Street. Free on Friday, Saturday and Sunday at 8:15 P.M., JU 6-4800 for information.

New York Shakespeare Festival — Delacourte Theatre, Central Park. Every night except Monday. Performance begins at 8:00 P.M. but get there before 6:00 P.M. to be assured tickets.

Pageant Players, The 6th Street Theatre Group and other street theatre groups perform on various street corners, particularly on the Lower East Side. Free Theatre is also provided at the **United Nations** building and the **Stock Exchange** on Wall Street, if you enjoy seventeenth century comedy.

If you look relatively straight you can sneak into conventions and get all kinds of free drinks, snacks and samples. Call the **New York Convention Bureau,** 90 East 42nd Street, MU 7-1300 for information. You can also get free tickets to theatre events here at 9:00 A.M.

FREE MOVIES — **New York Historical Society** — Central Park West and 77th Street. Hollywood movies every Saturday afternoon. Call TR 3-3400 for schedule.

Metropolitan Museum of Art — Fifth Avenue and 82nd Street. Art films Mondays at 3:00 P.M. Call TR 9-5500 for schedule.

New York University — Has a very good free movie program as well as poetry, lectures, and theatre presentations. Call the Program Director's Office, 598-2026 for schedule.

Millenium Film Workshop — 2 East 2nd Street. Fridays beginning at 7:15 P.M. open screening of films by underground directors.

This is our favorite way to sneak into a regular movie theatre: Arrive just as the show is emptying out and join the line leaving the theatre. Exclaiming, "Oh, my gosh!" slap your forehead, turn around and return, telling the usher you left your hat, pocketbook, etc., inside. Once you're in the theatre just take a seat and wait for the next show. Another method is to call the theatre early and pose as a film critic for one of the mini magazines and ask to be placed on the "O. K. list." Usually this works.

17

This works very well at pre-released screenings. You can phone the various screening studios and find out what they are screening.

FREE MUSIC — **Greenwich House of Music School** — 46 Barrow Street (of Seventh Avenue), West Village. Fridays at 8:30 P.M. Classical.
Donnell Library Center — 20 West 53rd Street. Schedule found in "Calendar of Events" at any library. Classical.

Frick Museum — 1 East 70th Street. BU 8-0700. Concerts every Sunday afternoon. The best of the classical offerings. You must do some red tape work though. Send self - addressed stamped envelope that will arrive on Monday before the date you wish to go. One letter — one ticket.

The Group Image — Performs every Wednesday night at the Hotel Diplomat on West 43rd Street between Sixth and Seventh Avenues, and you can get in free if you say you have no money (sometimes). If you promise to take your clothes off it's definitely free. If you ball on the dance floor, you get a season's pass.

Filmore East — 105 Second Avenue. If you live in the Lower East Side you can generally get into the Fillmore East after the show has started, if there are seats. Just go up to the door with a half way decent story. You're with the diggers or Evo or something will generally work.

There are various free festivals put on in Central Park. You can call the **City Parks Departments** for a schedule at 734-1000.

Washington Square in the West Village is always jumping on Sunday. Check out the Banana Singers either here or on St. Mark's Place. Cop a kazoo in Woolworths or a tambourine and join the band.

★ ★ ★

FREE MUSEUMS — **Metropolitan Museum** — Fifth Avenue and 82nd Street.

Frick Museum — 1 East 70th Street. Great when you're stoned. Closed Mondays.

The Cloisters — Weekdays 10 A.M. to 5 P.M., Sundays 1 P.M. to 6 P.M. Take IND Eighth Avenue express (A train) to 190th Street station and walk a few blocks. The #4 Fifth Avenue bus also goes all the way up and it's a pleasant ride. One of the best trip places in town in medieval setting.

Brooklyn Museum — Eastern Parkway and Washington Avenue. Egyptian stuff best in the world outside of Egypt. Take IRT (Broadway Line) express train to Brooklyn Museum station.

Museum of the American Indian — Broadway at 155th Street. The largest Indian museum in the world. Open Tuesday to Sunday 1 to 5 P.M. Take IRT (Broadway Line) local to 157th Street station.

Museum of Natural History — Central Park West and 79th Street. Great dinosaurs and other stuff. Weekdays 10 - 5 P.M., Sunday 1 - 5 P.M.

The Hispanic Society of America — Broadway between 15th and 156th Streets. The best Spanish art collection in the city.

Asia House Gallery — 112 East 64th Street. Art objects from the Far East.

Marine Museum of the Seaman's Church — 25 South Street. All kinds of model ships and sea stuff.

Chase Manhattan Bank Museum of Money — 1256 Sixth Avenue. Free people consider property as theft and regard all banks, especially Chase Manhattan ones, as museums.

★ ★ ★

THE STATEN ISLAND FERRY — Not free, but a nickel each way for a five mile ocean voyage around the southern tip of Manhattan is worth it. Take IRT (Broadway Line) to South Ferry, local only. Ferry leaves every half hour day and night.

★ ★ ★

FREE CRICKET MATCHES — At both Van Cortland Park in the Bronx and Walker Park on Staten Island every Sunday afternoon. Get schedule from British Travel Association, 43 West 61st Street. At Walker Park free tea and crumpets are served during intermission.

FREE POETRY, LECTURES, ETC. — The best advice here is to see the back page of the Village Voice for free events that week. There are a variety of talks given at the **Free School**, 20 East 14th Street. Call 675-7424 for information. For free brochures about free cultural events in New York go to **Cultural Information Center**, 148 West 57th Street.

FREE SWIMMING POOLS
1. — East 23rd Street and Asser Levy Place (near Avenue A). Indoor and outdoor pools, plus gymnasium.
2. — 83 Carmine Street (at Seventh Avenue, West Village). Indoor and outdoor pools plus gymnasium.
Bring your own swim suit and towel. 35c admission at certain times after 1:00 P.M. if you are over 14 years of age.

BRONX ZOO — Bronx and Pelham Parkways. Largest zoo in the U. S. Great collection of animals in natural settings. IRT Broadway (Dyre Avenue line) to 180th Street station and walk north. Free every day but Tuesday, Wednesday and Thursday when cost is 25c.
BOTANICAL GARDENS — 1000 Washington Avenue, Brooklyn. Another peaceful trip center. This and the Cloisters best in New York if you want to get away from it all quickly. Open 8:30 A.M. 'til dusk. Take IRT (Broadway line) to the Brooklyn Museum station.
FREE PARK EVENTS—All kinds of events in the Parks are free. Call 755-4100 for a recorded announcement of week's events.

★ ★ ★

You can get free posters, literature and books from the various missions to the United Nations located on the East Side near the U.N. building. The Cuban Mission, 6 E. 67th Street, will give you free copies of Granma, the Cuban newspaper, **Man and Socialism in Cuba**, a book by Che Guevara, and other literature. Ask for Mr. Jimenez.

You can get fingerprinted free and have your phone tapped at no expense by going to the F.B.I. at 201 East 69th Street. Call LE 5-7700, ask for J. Hoover. Tell him you're Walter Jenkins.

FREE PETS — **ASPCA,** 441 East 92nd Street and York Avenue. TR 6-7700. Dogs, cats, some birds and other pets. Tell them you're from out of town if you want a dog and you will not have to pay the $5.00 license fee. Have them inspect and innoculate the pet, which they do free of charge.

DRAFT RESISTANCE ADVICE — Many of you have problems that require draft counseling or maybe you have gone AWOL and need advice. There are numerous groups that will help out. Go down to 5 Beekman Street (near City Hall) and find your way to the 10th floor. There are many anti-draft groups located there who will give you the right kind of information. Call the **Resistance,** 732-4272 for details.

FREE CLOTHING REPAIRS — All Wallach stores feature a service that includes sewing on buttons, free shoe horns, and shoe laces, mending pants pockets and linings, punches extra holes in belts, and a number of other free services.

FREE CARS — If you want to travel a long distance the auto transportation agencies are a great deal. Look in the Yellow Pages under Automobile Transportation and Trucking. You must be over 21 and have a valid driver's license. Call them up and tell them when and where you want to go and they will tell you if they have a car. They give you the car and a tank of gas free. You pay the rest. Go to pick up the car alone, then get some people who also want to go to help with expenses. You can make San Francisco for about $80.00 in tolls and gas in four days without pushing. Usually you have the car for longer and can make a whole thing out of it. You must look "straight" when you go to the agency.

★ ★ ★

If you would like to meet a real ghost, write Hans Holzer c/o New York Committee for Investigation of Paranormal Research, 140 Riverside Drive, New York, N. Y. He'll put you in touch for free.

★ ★ ★

RADIO FREE NEW YORK — WBAI-FM, 99.5 on your dial, 30 East 39th Street, OX 7-2288, after midnight radio station provides air time for free souls who need help or offer it.

★ ★ ★

NEW YORK SCENES, a magazine, has a monthly column called "The Free Loader" with good advice on getting stuff free.

★ ★ ★

MIMEOGRAPH MACHINE — Both the ESSO office and Yippie have a free mimeo machine that you can use to print poetry, criticism, your life story or anything else.

★ ★ ★

FREE BAKERY — Every Wednesday some people get together and cook bread at St. Mark's Church on the Bowerie, Second Avenue and 10th Street.

★ ★ ★

Write to major corporations and tell them you bought one of their products and it doesn't work, or it shits, or it tastes bad. Most firms will send you up to a case of merchandise just to get you off their back. Try Tootsie Roll, Campbell's Soup and cigarette companies for starters. Also General Mills for cereals. Write to their public relations office. One day at the library and a few stamps will get you tons of stuff.

★ ★ ★

CLAP AND THE TASMANIAN PIG FEVER — Clap (syphilis and

22

gonorrhea) and Tasmanian Pig Fever (TPF) are two diseases you can easily pick up for free on the Lower East Side. One, the Clap, you catch, and the other, TPF, catches you. The Clap comes from balling. There are some that claim they get it from sitting on a toilet seat but that is possible only if you dig that position. Generally, using a prophylactic will prevent the spreading of Clap. If you don't use them and you ball a lot your chances of picking it up are pretty good. Syphilis usually begins with a sore which may look like a cold sore or any other kind of sore or pimple around your sex organ. Soon the sore disappears, even without treatment, and is often followed by an inflamation of the mouth and throat, and rashes on the body. These symptoms also disappear without any treatment. But even if these outer signs disappear the disease remains if untreated. If it remains untreated years later syphilis can cause serious trouble such as heart disease, blindness, insanity, and paralysis.

Gonorrhea is more common than syphilis. The first sign of gonorrhea is a discharge from your sex organ. It may not be noticed in women. In men there is usually itching and burning of the affected areas. If untreated it can result in permanent damage to sex glands. Both syphilis and gonorrhea can be cured in a short time with proper medical attention. The doctor's instructions must be followed to the letter if you want to shake the disease. Sometimes someone will get a shot of penicillin, go home and wait three days, and seeing no change in his condition he will assume the treatment is not working and not go back for more. Some strains are resistant to penicillin but will respond to other medication. Keep going to the clinic until the doctor says No. Free Treatment regardless of age is available for Lower East Side residents at the **Chelsea Hygiene Center**, 303 Ninth Avenue at 27th Street. Call LA 4-2537 for more free information. You can also gets tests for a variety of other illnesses here, including hepatitis, which is common and dangerous. Free cancer check-ups also given. Day and night phone information at 269-5300.

Tasmanian Pig Fever is a disease common to the Lower

East Side. It's the **cops.** You are liable to get busted for a variety of reasons. Let's face it, the Lower East Side is a ghetto and getting busted by a cop is common in any American ghetto. The following is some general basic advice and some help on the chief causes for busts — dope and runaways, although runaways are not technically busted.

The TPF is the riot control squad in New York and is called out to handle many street demonstrations. The local police come out of the Ninth Precinct located on 5th Street between First and Second Avenues. The local cops are under the direction of Lieutenant Joe Fink. There are numerous arrests down here and a working knowledge of what to do about the cops can be very helpful.

Never let cops in your house if they do not have a search warrant. Ask them to slip it under the door. They only have a right to enter without a search warrant if they have strong reason to believe a crime is being committed on the premises. Most cases without a search warrant are thrown out of court. If you are arrested, give your name and address. If you do not you will have bail trouble. You can give a friend's address. Do not discuss any details of your case with the police. Demand to see your lawyer (See Free Legal Aid Section). You are allowed a phone call and generally they will give you three. Call your closest friend and tell him you are arrested. He should be instructed to meet you in court at **100 Centre Street.** On the fourth floor your friend can find out what courtroom you will appear in for arraignment. There is a Legal Aid lawyer in the courtroom who will handle the arraignment. If the charges are misdemeanors he should be used; if the charges are felonies you might be advised to get help from a private lawyer, Mobilization for Youth or some other agency. A good lawyer can get a bail reduction that can save you a good deal of time if you are hard up for bread. Bail depends on a variety of factors ranging from previous arrests to the judge's hangover. It can be put up in collateral, i.e. a bank book, or often there is a cash alternative offered which amounts to about 10 to 20% of the bail. Try and have your friend show up with at least a hundred dollars in cash. For very high bail there are the bail bondsmen in the area of the courthouse who will cover the bail for a fee not to exceed 5%. You will need what they term a solid citizen to sign the bail papers and perhaps put up some collateral.

DOPE BUSTS — Possession of less than a quarter of an ounce of pot is considered a misdemeanor. The penalty can be up to one year. In actuality, a conviction for possession is very rare. The New York courts are quite lenient on this charge. More than a quarter of an ounce is considered possession with intent to sell. This along with sale (to an agent) are considered felonies and punishable by terms of up to 15 years in prison. A few precautions are in order. If you are carrying when busted eat it as soon as it is cool. Never sell to someone you do not know. Never make a sale with two other people present. Agents always buy with another person or agent present as a witness. Never sell to anyone facing an indictment for they are subject to pressure. Undercover agents have some pretty interesting disguises. Black undercover cops are very hard to spot. Often undercover cops wear beards and moustaches but few, contrary to rumor, have very long hair. Long hair that takes a year to grow is not possible since agents are switched around and anyway long hair doesn't grow in Queens. Undercover cops always carry a gun so look out for that noticeable bulge or a jacket being worn on a hot day.

There is a new bill already passed, waiting for the governor's signature, that would upgrade the dope penalties, for example, sale of pot to a minor could get you up to life imprisonment. If this bill is passed and you are caught selling to a minor, pull out a gun and shoot the kid. You can only get 10-20 years for first degree manslaughter and can be paroled in 6 years. Acid and other dope, although against the law rarely result in busts and even less in convictions (heroin is another thing, of course). There are too many technicalities involved in analyzing the substance, many such as STP are not covered by the law. For this reason, they generally go after the grass unless there is a major production or sale involved.

RUNAWAYS — Laws governing runaways are equally ridiculous. Persons who look underage (under 16 for males, under 18 for females) can be stopped by a cop anytime and asked to produce identification. If you are underage or do not have identification to prove otherwise you can be brought to the police station. There your parents or guardian is called. If you have permission to be here they let you go, if not, your parents can pick you up there. If they don't want you, you can be sent to the Youth Detention House which is a very bad trip indeed. If you are a runaway, get fake identification and quick. People who put up runaways are subject to arrest for contributing to the delinquency for a minor. If you want to go home and need a contact or if you want to stay a few days in a good place call **Judson Memorial Church** in Washington Square, GR 7-0351. This is the first year this program has been in effect but the people running it are cool. If you don't want them to call your parents or the cops they assure us they will not. They can house and feed about twenty-five young people.

DEMONSTRATIONS — A word should be said about demonstrations. Demonstrations with large numbers of arrests rarely result in convictions. Lawyers inform us of the over 3,000 arrests in recent anti-war, yippie demonstrations, etc. there have been no convictions. This does not mean things couldn't change drastically but these are the facts up to now.

Remember when arrested give only your name and address. Demand a search warrant if they want to come into your pad. The only know cure for Tasmanian Pig Fever is revolution. Paranoids unite!

DOPE — As you probably know, most dope is illegal, therefore some risks are always involved in buying and selling. In the legal section we have discussed the selling problems. Now let us consider the problems involved in buying. Arrests are not a problem unless you are inside and happen to get caught in a raid on a major dealer. What is a major hazard is getting burned. The usual trick is to take your dough and just vanish, leaving you standing on the street. Another method is substituting oregano or parsely for grass, chewing tobacco as hash, and aspirin and barbiturates as acid. A general rule is no bread up front. If you're getting an ounce or more of grass you are entitled to sample it. Hash can also be sampled. If you're considering buying a large amount of acid, buy one tab for a sample and try it first. Another rule is to buy from a known dealer or a close friend.

Have you considered growing your own? Being a weed, grass is very easy to grow if it gets enough water and sun. Get your seeds together, travel over to Jersey or Staten Island, find a field and plant your seeds. Draw a furrow in the ground about half an inch deep and plant the seeds about two inches apart. Cover the seeds with soil and water the area. Returning every two weeks to tend your crop will be sufficient. No matter how high the shoots get they are smokeable if dried out but it is best to let them grow to maturity (when the flowers bloom). This takes three to four months depending on soil conditions and sunlight. With a little effort, you can grow kilos galore. Growing grass indoors is a big hassle but it can be done if you construct a planting box with a light bulb or artificial growing lamp. Some hardy souls have planted grass in Carl Schurz Park next to Gracie Mansion, 89th Street and East River Drive.

There are also legal highs, the most famous of which is bananas. Scrap the insides of the banana peel and roast in a 200° oven for a half hour or until dark brown. Crumble the scrapings and roll in a joint or pack in a pipe. This will produce a mild pot high.

Mornings glory seeds will produce a high similar to LSD if prepared properly. Use only the white, blue, or blue-white varieties that are not coated with chemicals. If they have been coated a good washing in alcohol will remove it. You need about 400 seeds to get you up there. Generally there are about 40 to 60 in a packet. We prefer the following method: grind the seeds in a pepper mill and stuff them into gelatin capsules that you can get in any drug store. Another method is to boil the seeds, strain the mixture and drink the liquid. It tastes bitter but it's easier than the grinding method. It's an 8-10 hour trip.

Whipped cream containers are 80% nitrous oxide or laughing gas. Hold the container upright and release the nozzle slowly as you inhale. It's really a gas; even the whipped cream gets you high.

Some people claim you can get high on cabbage centers. Others claim cigarette tobacco mixed with powdered aspirins will do the trick. A hint on grass: boil the twigs and seeds and make a very groovy tea — sort of a tea-tea.

BAD TRIPS — The best method for bringing a person down from a bad trip is calm, understanding talk by a sympathetic soul. Generally this works. Orange juice and sugar works well. A cup of sugar to a quart of orange juice. Drink as much as you can. **Niacinimide,** a vitamin B derivative also works. You need 1000 milligrams for every 100 micrograms of LSD. Say the tablets you have are 100 mg. That means ten tablets for each 100 micrograms of LSD. If you do not know the LSD dosage, assume 500 micrograms and use 50 tablets of Niacinimide. Too much Niacinimide cannot hurt you. Landing time for both the orange juice-sugar method and Niacinimide is between 30-40 minutes. Niacinimide has better results. It is available without a prescription and is fairly cheap. You can get a thousand tablets for about three dollars.

As a last resort you should call in a physician who can administer a tranquilizer, generally thorazine. Bellevue should be considered a bad trip.

Be careful of drugs you know nothing about. STP is only for people who have been into acid for a time. Heroin is addictive and can be a mighty expensive habit. Amphetamine, usually called A or meth or speed, is also quite dangerous if you don't know what you are doing. Both heroin and meth are self-destructive. They ruin your appetite, often causing malnutrition. Since they are needle drugs there is always the chance of missing a vein, which leads to a stiff arm for a few days or of contracting serum hepatitis from unsterilized needles. You can kick the habit by just refusing to take it for a few weeks or switching to a groovier drug. Don't get hooked on any drug, whether it be heroin, school, coca-cola, benzedrine, suburbia, meth, or politics. They can all rot your brain . . . Be advised.

COMMUNES — Communes can be a cheap and enjoyable way to live. They are a good tribal way to live in the city. Because they are tribes each has a personality of its own. This personality depends on the people in the commune and how well they get along together. For this reason the most important part of setting up a commune is choosing people who are compatible. It is vital that no member of the commune has any strong objection to any other member. More communes have been destroyed by incompatibility than any other single reason. People of similar interests (speed freaks with speed freaks, painters with painters, and revolutionaries with revolutionaries) should get together. Preferably the members of the commune should know each other before they begin setting up quarters.

Once there is a nucleus of 4 to 7 people that are compatible establishing a commune is not difficult. The first thing to do is rent an apartment. The initial cost will probably be two months rent. Don't pay more. The landlord is not legally allowed to ask for more than one month's rent as security. Don't go to a rental agency unless you are willing to pay an extra month's rent as a fee. Two ways you can find an apartment if you don't know of one are: walk up and down every street and look for rent signs; the other is to look inside the front doors of some buildings in the area for a sign giving the landlord's name. When you find buildings owned by one company there is a pretty good chance that the company owns other buildings in the area. Call that company and ask if they have any vacant apartments.

When you get an apartment, furnishing will be the next step. You can double your sleeping space by building loft or bunk beds. Nail two by fours securely from ceiling to floor about three feet from the walls where beds are wanted. Then build a frame out of two by fours at the height you want the beds. Make sure it is strong enough to hold the weight of people sleeping on it. Then nail a sheet of 3/4 inch plywood on the frame. Mattresses and other furniture can be gotten for free. See the section on free .furniture. You can cop silverware in self-service restaurants.

How you govern your commune depends on where the member's heads are. One method which works well is the Indian tribal council in which from time to time all members of the tribe (commune) get together and discuss problems that come up and solutions are worked out. At the meeting it should be decided which members are responsible for the things that have to be done (i. e. cooking cleaning, raising the rent); this assures that they will be done. It is a good idea to have a meeting when you first form to make decisions on some of the important things that are sure to arise. The first is whether you want a crash pad or a commune. The difference is that a commune is a closed unit. Other people may join, but unlike a crash pad, they may not join for one day. Other things to consider are drugs (no drugs in the pad, communal stash, etc.), property (personal, communal), age limits and so on. The important thing to remember is that with experience and basic trust for each other, this form of tribal living is by far the best way to live in the city jungle. Ask around for an experienced commune and get one of their members to come to your first tribal meeting. The more stable communes that are established the sooner we can begin to realize a freer more humanistic society.

Revolution is Free. Venceremos!

"America is the land of the Free.

My ol' man George always told me that

Free means you don't pay."

Jim Metesky

POSTSCRIPT

There is a rumor that the City of New York paid for the Book. The rumor is TRUE. I made a deal that I would never tell where the money came from and it was an honest deal. I can say it is true now because there is so much garbage spread out in this book that you are still not sure. Somewhere in New York in a safe-deposit box are photostatic copies of all the check transactions between the City of New York, the in-between party, and the printer. The Red Squad (Bureau of Special Services) knows all this and would like to use the evidence against Mayor Lindsay. If I ever get killed or convicted on serious charges in New York the photostatic copies go straight to the *Daily News*. *The duty of a revolutionist is to stay out of jail.*

* * * *

The Department of the Interior has received over 300 requests for free buffaloes, as well as some requests for free Yippies. Free buffaloes, they now say, can be given only to tax-exempt institutions such as zoos or orphanages. As for Yippies, according to their AP dispatch, "they are being placed on our list of endangered species."

* * * *

The address of YIP was printed in the *Village Voice* and we received over 3,000 requests for the Book, which we honored. The address also appeared in the *Daily News* and we received 8,000 requests, none of which will be honored. The *Daily News* called the Book "New York on No Dollars a Day," which, of course, we never heard of. It's always interesting to hear it referred to in the overground press because they always have to change its name.

The Book has been reprinted in the New York *Free Press,* mimeographed by a Bedford-Stuyvesant school teacher, and is being translated into Spanish. It has been favorably received all over the world. We would like to do a national edition.

*   *   *   *

The New York State drug law referred to in the book was recently vetoed.

*   *   *   *

Colonel John Masters of ICC no longer works in the Pentagon.

*   *   *   *

Many of the places that give free things away have been inundated with so many requests that they have changed their policy. The reader will have to shop around. The book was intended primarily for use in New York during the summer.

*   *   *   *

LNS has moved and Rappaport's has gone out of business. Not because of the free rolls, I hope.

*   *   *   *

FREE FLYING — In order to work this you need access to the mailbox of a person who is listed in the phonebook. Let's use the name Ron Davis as an example. Have a girl call one of the airlines with a rap similar to the following: "Hello, this is Mr. Davis' secretary at Allied Chemical. He and his wife would like to fly to Chicago on Friday. Could you mail two tickets to his home and bill us here at Allied?" Every major corporation probably has a Ron Davis working for them. The airline company doesn't bother checking anyway. Order your tickets two days before you wish to travel. Have a good flight! If you're nervous about using that trick always remember to try Youth Fare. If it wasn't for Youth Fare there would have been no Chicago. Thank you TWA for joining the conspiracy.

*   *   *   *

We gave away 15,000 copies of *Fuck the System* free. I can always tell a communist because he's the one with the plan for us to make money on the book.

The YIP office was closed a week before we left for Chicago.

ABOUT THE AUTHOR

One of the most influential and recognizable American activists of the twentieth century, Abbie Hoffman was born in 1936 in Worcester, Massachusetts. After graduating from Brandeis University in 1959 with a degree in psychology, Hoffman became active in the civil rights movement of the early 1960s. Along with many others determined to make a difference, he traveled to Mississippi to help register voters. In New York City, he founded Liberty House, a crafts store that sold goods made by cooperatives in Mississippi.

In the mid-1960s, Hoffman became an organizer in both the growing U.S. counterculture and the anti–Vietnam War movement. In his autobiography, Hoffman wrote: "A semi-structure freak among the love children, I was determined to bring the hippie movement into a broader protest." With his unique political wit and humor, and his awareness of television's growing importance in shaping social awareness, Hoffman helped organize such memorable acts of 1960s protest as dropping dollar bills onto the New York Stock Exchange in April 1967, and "levitating" the Pentagon in October of that same year. In 1968, together with his then-wife Anita, Jerry Rubin, Nancy Kurshan, Paul Krassner, and others, Hoffman founded the Youth International Party ("Yippies!") and began organizing a Festival of Life outside the Democratic Party's 1968 national convention in Chicago. Following what investigators later called a "police riot," Hoffman and seven others (the "Chicago 8") were put on trial in what became known as the Chicago Conspiracy Trial—"the most important political trial of this century" according to the ACLU.

In 1973, Hoffman went underground, and using alias names like Barry Freed still managed to stay politically active, working successfully with his "running mate" Johanna Lawrenson on Save the River!—a campaign that stopped the Army Corps of Engineers from dredging the St. Lawrence River for winter navigation. He emerged from the underground on national television in

September of 1980 and continued his work, in his own words, as "an American dissident and a community organizer" throughout the 1980s. His projects included working with environmental groups throughout the Great Lakes and the Northeast, taking delegations to Central America to question American policies in the region, and opposing workplace drug testing in the U.S.

Student activists gained much from Hoffman's experience—the veteran organizer dedicated considerable time and energy to passing along the skills he had developed. Arrested in 1986 with Amy Carter and other students at the University of Massachusetts while protesting CIA recruitment on campus, Hoffman yet again shaped a precedent-setting trial. Hoffman and the students successfully pleaded not guilty using the "necessity defense," convincing a jury that their minor crime of trespass was needed to stop larger crimes of CIA covert actions in Central America and elsewhere. In his closing argument, Hoffman told the jury: "I grew up with the idea that democracy is not something you believe in, or a place you hang your hat, but it's something you do. You participate. If you stop doing it, democracy crumbles and falls apart. . . . Young people, if you participate, the future is yours." Throughout the 1980s, Hoffman traveled extensively across the country to give lectures on college campuses and was the major adviser for such activist groups as National Student Convention '88 (at Rutgers University) and Student Action Union—helping student activists learn tools and strategies for building effective, democratically structured movements for social change.

Hoffman married three times, to Sheila Karklin, Anita Kushner, and Johanna Lawrenson. He had three children: Andrew and Ilya (with Sheila), and america (with Anita). He wrote seven books, including several classics that have since helped to define the culture and politics of his times.

Abbie Hoffman will forever be remembered as an activist who inspired young people to question authority, as an American radical who introduced humor and theater into political organizing, and as an embodiment of a hopeful era in which millions of people throughout the globe embraced their democratic potential to help create a better world.

PHOTO COURTESY OF JOHANNA LAWRENSON

Abbie and Johanna Lawrenson, wife, co-organizer, and running mate, with Randy Borman on Rio Aqua Rico, Headwaters of the Amazon, Equador, January 1986. Abbie and Johanna got together in Mexico in the spring of 1974 while Abbie was underground. From 1974 until Abbie's death in 1989, they worked on numerous environmental projects, Central American anti-intervention issues, and CIA campus recruitment policies, as well as other student movements. Today, Johanna is president of the Abbie Hoffman Activist Foundation.